Creating a Prospering Practice
Spending Little or No Money Marketing

By Linda Steele, CMT

ISBN 0-7414-1796-0

Published by:

PUBLISHING.COM

519 West Lancaster Avenue
Haverford, PA 19041-1413
Info@buybooksontheweb.com
www.buybooksontheweb.com
Toll-free (877) BUY BOOK
Local Phone (610) 520-2500
Fax (610) 519-0261

Printed in the United States of America

Printed on Recycled Paper

Published January 2004

Table of Contents

This book is dedicated to Elaine O'Regan, a wonderful woman
who treated me like her daughter and
supported me in all my ventures.   She left this world
way too soon and she is truly missed.

Acknowledgements

The material in this book is a compilation of knowledge I have gained throughout my life. To name all those who contributed to my understanding of this material would be quite impossible. So I would like to express my deep gratitude collectively to the teachers, mystics, gurus and philosophers who have left a legacy of their wisdom in books and on tapes so that we may benefit from their experiences.

I also would like to acknowledge my close friends, MaryAnn Sanders and Kerri Burkey. They gave helpful advice on the manuscript itself, but more than that, their belief in me and the material gave me confidence and strength.

I would also like to acknowledge and thank my coaches Lorri Bein and Nina East. Their encouragement gave me insight when I was stuck.

Stan Barrett, my former boss, at DocuPro, also deserves special thanks. He taught me a lot about marketing, business and going after my dreams.

And last but not least, I would like to thank my editor Mary McClurkin (you can reach her at www.neweyesediting.com). She was fabulous to work with and honored my timeline for finishing this book.

Introduction

When I was in massage school, I knew I wanted to write a book about marketing. It was a subject that was sorely lacking in our education, especially for those who wanted to start their own practices. In fact, marketing was scarcely mentioned.

As I was planning my business and developing my business plan, writing a book became part of it, and after I started my practice in 2000 I was convinced of the need for it. Clients and other massage therapists often remarked that they were impressed with the growth of my business in such a short period of time.

I developed a plan to start writing this book after my first year in business. My original intention was to write a book on marketing in general, including the statistics from each method I tried during that first year. I finished the book in October 2001, my first anniversary in business, and I started sending the manuscript to publishers.

As I went about that process, I happened in to a bookstore, found myself scanning the Alternative Health section and saw a book called *Marketing Massage* by Monica Roseberry. My first thought was that I was "a day late and a dollar short." I flipped through her book and read a few sections.

Some of what she said I didn't agree with but I began to have second thoughts about the content of my book. The reason was that there are a lot of great marketing books out there, so why repackage that information here.

I began to wonder how I could differentiate this book from others on the market. The result is the content you are about to read. What is does that is different is tell you:

- the steps I used to create my vision and my marketing plan and how you can do the same thing.
- the marketing methods I used, why I used them, whether I would use them again.
- pitfalls to look out for, and
- the steps I used to reduce the amount of money I was spending on marketing efforts after the first year while increasing sales and building my business every month.

This book is written both for those who are already in business but would like to start a marketing plan as well as those who are thinking about going into business and want to start out on the right foot.

While I can't guarantee you success, I think you will find several useful nuggets of information that will get you on the right track. I would consider this book a great success, if every massage therapist who reads it can take at least one piece of information and use it in their business to help them grow their practices.

Linda Steele

Chapter 1
Creating Your Vision

Before you can create a vision of what you want your business to become, you will have to understand what marketing is all about. It is not the combative "advertising" so many people associate with it. Rather, it can take many forms – many of them comfortable and familiar.

So What is Marketing Anyway?

Many massage therapists cringe at the term. They are professionals, and professionals don't "market" themselves because they provide a service that enhances a person's health and well-being. Are you one of those? Well, I am here to tell you that you shouldn't be afraid of marketing. Everyone markets every day, in our work and even in our personal lives. We market ourselves to potential friends, the one we seek as our life mate, or to gain a position that we really want.

Since we are not dealing with our individual lives but with our business or one we are about to start, I will give you a different perspective on marketing as well as a different definition of it. Simply put: Marketing is any method that encourages potential clients to come to you for your services.

There is an endless variety of marketing tools to promote a business. There are no-cost and low-cost methods such as: word-of-mouth, referral incentives, business cards, brochures, and direct mail. Newspaper and telephone directory advertising and Web sites represent a somewhat greater investment. High cost methods are radio and television ads. With all of these choices, how do you decide which ones to choose? The answer: Your marketing plan should be aligned with the scope of your vision. And that vision is the first thing you should determine.

Creating Your Vision

First, you need to have a clear idea of what you want your marketing to do for you. When you picture yourself as successful, what do you see? I can't tell you this because your definition of success is different from mine. Are you happy having ten clients a week? Or is maybe 20 enough? Do you want all of your treatment rooms fully booked seven days a week?

No one has that vision but you. And you must know what it is so you can see if your plan will work the way you want it to.

So right now, take the time to write out exactly what you want. It is important to *write* it down because writing creates the energy that transforms thought into action and gives your subconscious mind the ability to make it happen for you.

Here are the ground rules:

1. Write only what you want, not what anyone else *wants* you to want or *thinks* you should want.
2. Do this when you are in a positive state of mind. Find the right time. You may want to meditate first to get there.
3. Write what you want in the present tense--as if it were already reality.
4. Assume that you cannot fail. Remember that you are writing it in the present tense, so if you already have it, how could you fail?

Go ahead. Dare to dream!

_____

_____

_____

_____

_____

_____

_____

_____

Now that you have your vision, let's explore how your marketing plan is going to make it a reality.

Chapter 2
Marketing Plan

What is a Marketing Plan, and why do you need one?

A Marketing Plan is a concise set of steps that shows your business goals and the methods you are going to use to achieve them. You need a marketing plan because it helps to improve your company's focus. There is an old saying: "Whatever you focus on, you get". So if you are focusing on your goals clearly and concisely, you are more likely to be successful than if you aren't.

If you don't have a marketing plan because you have never bothered to create one or are a fledgling business, now is the time to make a new start. Here are seven points of a good marketing plan with a sample of each. Each consists of one to two sentences to serve as a possible model for your work. I adopted this information from Jay Conrad Levinson's book *Guerrilla Marketing.* Following this section, you will find space to create your own marketing plan.

Creating a Marketing Plan

1. State the purpose of your marketing plan.

The purpose of my marketing plan is to serve as a guide in keeping us focused on our goals.

2. Tell how this purpose will be achieved by the benefits of your offering.

By using our chosen marketing tools, we will add 370 customers per year (or increase sales by 25% per year).

3. Define your target market. Who do you want as clients? You must pick a target market in order to give you focus. I have found that some people think that a target market is limiting their business. This is not the case. A target market gives you a group to concentrate your marketing efforts towards. My target market is 30-60 year olds within a three-mile radius, but I can tell you I have clients that are younger as well as older and come from all over.

We will cater to 30-60 year olds within a three-mile radius of MassageWorks.

4. Describe your proposed marketing tools.

We will use brochures, business cards, word-of-mouth advertising, newspaper ads, the telephone directory and marketing alliances.

5. What is your niche? (A niche differentiates your business from your competitors. The following are sample niches: quality, service, speed, convenience, experience, low prices, innovation or selection.)

Our niche is high quality service giving added selection to our clients with convenience a must.

6. Explain your company's identity, the way you would like customers to think of your business.

MassageWorks' identity is one of concern for our clients, always listening to their needs and wants and tailoring our services to fit these specifications.

7. Describe your marketing budget expressed as a percent of your projected gross sales.

We will devote 10% of projected gross sales to our marketing effort.

Now Create Your Own Marketing Plan

State the purpose of your marketing plan.

_____

_____

_____

_____

_____

How will you achieve your goal?

_____
_____
_____
_____
_____

Define your target market.

_____
_____
_____
_____
_____

Describe your proposed marketing tools.

_____
_____
_____
_____
_____

Describe your niche.

_____
_____
_____
_____
_____

Explain your company's identity.

_____
_____
_____
_____
_____

Describe your marketing budget expressed as a percent of your projected gross sales.

For easy reference, you may want to type this marketing plan and put in the same binder as your business plan.

How to Use Your Marketing Plan

Now that you have your marketing plan written what do you do with it? This plan should be used as a benchmark to judge whether a particular method achieves your company's marketing goals.

Marketing Plan Maintenance

Review your marketing plan at least once each year and compare it with the results from each of your marketing methods. In order to compare the results you got from each marketing tool compared to your plan, you'll have to have a way to track how your clients came to you. A good way to keep track of what clients came from what source is QuickBooks. In every customer record, there is a box for Referral Source.

If you are new in business or just instituting a marketing plan, I would suggest that you might want to review your plan more frequently. For the first couple of years, you may want to have a quarterly review. If the marketing methods you have chosen don't meet your criteria, or if your criteria needs to be changed as your business evolves, make those changes as necessary. How do you know if you need to change things? I will give you an example from my business.

I advertised with the *Sun Gazette* bi-weekly at a rate of $187. After several quarterly reviews, I realized that I had advertised a total of 14 times, but my payback was only 14 clients. On the other hand, my payback with the *Falls Church News Press* was 42 clients, which only cost $49 per submission. I felt I had given the *Gazette* publication a fair shot and decided to discontinue.

Another reason to use and stay committed to your plan is that you will receive countless calls and mailings offering you "a sure-fire way" to get clients into your door. Remember that the people who are calling are very good at their job, so resist. If it isn't in your plan, don't do it. I am not saying you should never add anything new. If your marketing plan is up for review and you want to try another marketing method that you think may be viable by all means add it.

Chapter 3
Getting Started

Where Do I Begin?

Now that you have your marketing plan you will need to devise a marketing calendar.

Marketing Calendar

One of my aims in writing this book is to provide you with tips so you don't have to experience the same mistakes I made. Having said that let me tell you about my mistake of not implementing a marketing calendar and the reason one is so essential.

A few therapists I talked to before I started my business said that it would be hard work to have a fully functioning successful business and take some time to build a steady clientele. So when I first opened my doors for business, I thought I would have that time to build a steady clientele and get things done like finishing my Web site and hiring therapists.

However, I was full of energy and wanted to be successful as quickly as possible. I visualized a busy successful practice and went about instituting all the methods described in my marketing plan with the exception of my Web site and the Yellow Pages listing.

You know that saying, "Be careful what you wish for; you just may get it." Well that happened to me, and I was not prepared. I was busy from the day I opened my doors. I was the only one doing the work, as I had not hired additional therapists or a receptionist. Thankfully my mom was there to help with the phones and to get the general office paperwork set up. I was literally working 12-15 hours a day, seven days a week and still had to turn people away. When I was not seeing clients, I was doing research on my Web site because it was my goal to have it up and running by December 1 so I could have exposure for selling gift certificates during the holidays. I honestly didn't even have time to interview anyone until December 24 (almost five months after opening my business).

After that I stopped listening to what "everyone" says will happen, and I go for what I want.

Being Prepared

I would strongly recommend that you devise a marketing calendar. Include in it what you will do and when. Then post this timeline where you can see it so you can avoid costly mistakes. I would suggest implementing several marketing methods each quarter: one to three "no-cost," one or two "low-cost," and depending on your budget, one "medium-cost".

Once you have created your vision and marketing plan, let's look at the methods I used and why I used them. I will also share some of the pitfalls I ran into while using these marketing methods.

Over the next several chapters, I will detail the methods that I used and the rationale for doing so, the possible pitfalls, and recommendations for future use.

Chapter 4

"No-cost Marketing"

Who Do You Know?

My first plan of attack was to let my friends, family and acquaintances know, if they didn't already, that I was now in the massage therapy business. First, I wrote an introductory letter and set about getting business cards, brochures and discount postcards made, which does require a moderate outlay of money. My intention was to send this packet (with three business cards, brochures and postcards) to each person on my mailing list.

Word-of-mouth

Word-of-mouth is anything you and your clients can do to spread the word about your business. By far, this will be your most effective marketing method provided you give consistent quality and service.

Why? There are several reasons:

You have instant rapport and trust built within your circle of influence (people you know).

Satisfied customers will become repeat clients.

Repeat clients spread the word and provide the referrals that are cost-free marketing. Of the 18 people whose referrals I can trace, I have had 181 new customers. So it is easy to see if you give the quality and consistency of service, your business will begin to grow almost by itself.

Keep in mind that if you are not providing top quality service, "word-of-mouth" can be disastrous. Statistics show that a satisfied customer will tell one to three people, but a dissatisfied customer will tell 10-12. Often, you will not even know the customer has been dissatisfied with your service until the negative publicity has done its work.

Let me illustrate this point with a real life example that happened to me. I bought a Palm Pilot from a local retailer in November 2000 because I was so busy I wanted to get myself organized. Even then I didn't have time to put all of my information in it until about a month after I purchased it. A short time after that I went to use my Palm and there was no data. Thinking I might have done something wrong, I reentered the data. After entering all this information for a second time, the Palm dumped it again. I thought this Palm must surely be defective.

I went back to the store to see if I could exchange it. Since I didn't buy the maintenance contract, they were not willing to help me. I even spoke to the manager. His reply was "There is nothing I can do."

Having been a manager before, I know that you can *always* do something if you really want to keep a customer. Furthermore, I am relatively young and I intend to continue to buy electronics, but I will not buy anything at that store.

Of course I told everyone who would listen about my experience. And those people probably told more people. As we learned earlier, favorable word-of-mouth spreads slowly unless you accelerate it. It takes attention and effort. So right now, write down of the following lines at least 100 people that you will send an introductory packet to.

Here are some of the areas that I considered my circle of influence: friends, immediate family, relatives who live close by, people in aerobics classes and other classes and workshops I attended, neighbors, former co-workers, hair stylists, doctors, dentist, associations to which I belong. Others could be church, school, parents of your kid's friends, and salespeople with whom you do regular or occasional business.

The Who Do I Know List

1	_____	18	_____
2	_____	19	_____
3	_____	20	_____
4	_____	21	_____
5	_____	22	_____
6	_____	23	_____
7	_____	24	_____
8	_____	25	_____
9	_____	26	_____
10	_____	27	_____
11	_____	28	_____
12	_____	29	_____
13	_____	30	_____
14	_____	31	_____
15	_____	32	_____
16	_____	33	_____
17	_____	34	_____

35 _____	68 _____
36 _____	69 _____
37 _____	70 _____
38 _____	71 _____
39 _____	72 _____
40 _____	73 _____
41 _____	74 _____
42 _____	75 _____
43 _____	76 _____
44 _____	77 _____
45 _____	78 _____
46 _____	79 _____
47 _____	80 _____
48 _____	81 _____
49 _____	82 _____
50 _____	83 _____
51 _____	84 _____
52 _____	85 _____
53 _____	86 _____
54 _____	87 _____
55 _____	88 _____
56 _____	89 _____
57 _____	90 _____
58 _____	91 _____
59 _____	92 _____
60 _____	93 _____
61 _____	94 _____
62 _____	95 _____
63 _____	96 _____
64 _____	97 _____
65 _____	98 _____
66 _____	99 _____
67 _____	100 _____

You should try to fill in all 100 names, but if you can't, don't worry about it. Remember you can return to this list and add names as they occur to you.

Your Introductory Letter

If you are just starting your business you can write a letter that introduces you and your business. Here is the letter I sent to those on my "Who Do I Know" list.

Dear Friends

In March 2000, I finished massage school, passed my national certification exam, and I am now a certified massage therapist in Virginia. I have decided to open my own massage practice. I will be open for business on October 20, 2000. It is called MassageWorks, Inc. and it will be located at 450 W. Broad Street, Suite 412, Falls Church, Virginia 20046. The telephone number is (703) 536-7200.

I need your help to get my business going. I am including a few brochures, business cards and discount coupons. If you could give them to people you know who may need a good massage I would greatly appreciate it. Be sure to let me know if you need any more cards or brochures.

I hope you see you in my office soon.

If you are already in practice but would like to increase your referral rate, you can write a letter to your existing client base asking them for help to grow your business. Ask them to refer their friends and co-workers to you if they were happy with your service. Be sure to tell them about your referral plan. You can give them 10% off their next visit or a free gift for any referral who has had a session with you.

My Experience with Word-of-mouth

I also call this area my circle of influence. From word-of-mouth alone, the following business was generated.

Percentage of Clients:	26%
Percentage of Income:	33%
Percentage of Advertising:	0
Cost Per Client:	$0

At the beginning of this chapter, I said that word-of-mouth marketing would far exceed all of the rest in terms of income to expense. I think my statistics have proven this statement. Word-of-mouth ranks first in income generation and exceeds the next closest method, the Yellow Pages, by 58%. Whew! It also ranks first in number of clients.

Would I use this method again? I think you know my answer to this one. I would absolutely positively use word-of-mouth advertising. I would also try to think of other people I knew or ways to meet more of them.

Chapter 5

"Low-cost" Marketing

The methods I determined as "low-cost" is the use of collateral materials (i.e. business cards, brochures, letterhead, invoices, etc.) where design and printing costs are the only costs involved. Other possibilities could be post cards and flyers and referral incentives.

My Experience with "Low-cost" Advertising

Percentage of Clients: 8.3%
Percentage of Income: 13%
Percentage of Advertising: 3.6%
Cost Per Client: $5.26

I have lumped all of the ways that I have used business cards, brochures, post cards and flyers together with the exception of my circle of influence.

Income from "low-cost" marketing ranks #3. The only costs associated with this method are minimal printing costs. While less than 10% of the clients come from this method, income per client is high at $305 per person. The only actual work involved is making sure the distribution locations are continually stocked with your information. I keep a stock of collateral materials in my car, so that when I am at the grocery store, yoga studio, or other places that have agreed to display my material, I can replenish their supply as necessary. There is no question I would do this again.

Business Cards

Business cards are powerful reminders of you and your business. At the very least your business cards should contain the following information: (1) your name (2) your company name (3) your complete address (4) your telephone number and (5) your Web site URL.

Definitely have your business cards displayed in your waiting area, on your desk for easy reach, and possibly in your treatment room. At the end of a new client's session, have two business cards ready for him or her to take. Explain that one is to keep and one to give to someone else whom could benefit from massage.

The following is a list of DOs and DON'Ts I have learned in various arenas: college, my previous career and seminars I have attended.

DOs

Be creative so your card will standout. Most cards are horizontal. Be different; make your card vertical.
Create and use a logo.
Use high quality stock.
Check the proof for typos.

DON'Ts

Don't cross out old information. Business cards are relatively inexpensive to print. So, when you have outdated information, get new cards printed. It'll make you look more professional.
Don't forget to take them everywhere you go.
Don't use the "do it yourself" kind that are available at office supply stores. The reason for this is that people can feel the perforations and know you did the printing on your laser jet. It can make you look cheap.

Brochures

Most people will not go to the trouble of picking up and reading a brochure unless they are seriously interested in gaining information about a particular business or service. So here is your chance to give all of the pertinent information that will set you and your business apart from your competition.

Brochures are easy to change, especially if you create your own using one of the software packages mentioned below. They are also inexpensive to print. I paid $400 for 5000 when I first started in business and three years later I probably have about 500 left.

Some valuable suggestions for creating your brochure.

Have your brochure professionally designed. If you can't afford the additional cost, you can create your own in many of the software packages such as MSWord or Publisher, and PrintShop.

Before you create your own brochure or have someone do it for you, do your research by looking at other brochures both in the massage industry and others.

Consider using a tri-fold brochure that can either fit into a business envelope or serve as a self-mailer (a brochure printed double-sided with one of the panels reserved for your return address in the upper left-hand corner and a space for the client address). My brochure was designed as a self-mailer in order to eliminate the cost of envelopes.

As a cost-saving measure, print in black and white.

Create brochures that can be used for years. Instead of writing "The business is three years old," write "We were founded in 2000." With this in mind, don't include your fees in your brochure as they will surely go up along with the costs of doing business. Instead create a separate card (or tri-fold document) called a "Menu of Services" that can be changed easily should your prices or services change.

Things to include in your brochure

Introduction to Massage Therapy
Benefits of Massage
Modalities
About the owner. I have included the following statement in my brochure, "Linda Steele, CMT, is the owner of MassageWorks, Inc. and a member of the NCBTMB and ABMP. She is a graduate of Virginia Learning Institute for Massage. She continues to increase her skills and bodywork techniques through continuing education seminars and workshops. Linda is a Reiki Master/Teacher. She offers sessions and classes to those interested in this technique."

Mission Statement: "Our mission is to revitalize your body, mind and spirit as we produce an environment that is focused on your well-being. We will bestow superior customer care while maintaining a harmonious relationship with the environment."

About our therapists. If you have other therapists working for you, you may want to include something similar to the following statement, "All therapists are certified by the NCBTMB, licensed (or certified by your state), and are members of either AMTA, ABMP or IMA."

Hours of Operation. I would avoid listing specific days and hours open, but put something like "Open seven days a week, by appointment only."

Information on tipping. Since massage is relatively new compared to other industries where tipping is standard, some people just don't know and are often embarrassed to ask. I included the following statement in my brochure "Tipping is always left to the discretion of our clients."

Getting brochures in the hands of prospects

Mail brochures to those on your prospect list. Remember *The Who Do I Know List* in Chapter 4. Also add anyone who requests a brochure to your prospect list.

Place them where potential clients frequent: health food stores, yoga or Pilates studios, gyms, community bulletin boards in grocery stores, libraries, etc.

You should also have a separate client list. You may want to routinely mail brochures to your client base so that they can pass them along to their friends or relatives.

Place your brochures in your waiting area.

Special Client-only Brochure

You may also want to create a special brochure to be given to clients only. These brochures can help your clients put the right words in their mouths when they talk about their massage experience.

Post Cards

Post cards are inexpensive to mail and can be created in-house. Create a post card that offers a discount, for example.

DOs

Create a professional-looking design, especially if done in-house;

Use compelling headline words in large type;

Use full-color graphics and print.

Suggestions for using postcards

Give a certain percentage (i.e. 10-15%) or dollar amount (i.e. $10).

Create a special post card for clients to give out. You can tell existing clients that you are striving to build your business and that you would appreciate their help. Ask them to give the post cards to their family, friends and business associates and you will give them their referral discount each time one of their post cards comes back. A simple way of knowing who was responsible for that post card is to devise a special number (i.e. Joe Doe would be D101) and put it on the lower right hand corner of each post card.

Offer a post card tailored to pregnant women. You can ask local OB/GYNs to put them in their patients' "new mother packets." More about this in the "Marketing Alliances" section.

DON'Ts

Let the offer go on forever. You want to create a sense of urgency. If the post card never expires, your prospects might just say "I'll make an appointment next week" and never get around to it.

Let your post card go out with any errors at all. Proofread your work. If you are doing the work in-house, have someone else proofread your work.

My Experience with Post cards

In October 2000 I created a post card offering 15% off the first visit. It expired December of that year.

I mailed the postcards to my prospect list and well as put them in the following places: the lobby of our building, the post office, a yoga studio, two health food stores, a local dry cleaners. I also gave them out at trade shows, health fairs and lectures.

I did a second printing of the postcards that offered only 10% off in September 2002 and I had them printed at Kinkos for a few hundred dollars.

With the second offer, I basically doubled the number of clients but tripled the number of referrals. The percentage of income and clients may be less than 1% of their totals, but I would definitely use this marketing method again. Why? Because the advertising costs are inexpensive, and the cards are something I can give to prospective clients.

Flyers

A flyer's primary goal is to make a special offer, one that creates a sense of urgency (Tie it to a holiday or other event, and remember to include an expiration date). Be sure to include all of your pertinent information (business name, address, and phone number). You may also want to include whether your accept credit cards and your hours of operation. Distinguish it by printing it on colored paper.

Flyers are less expensive than brochures because they can be designed in-house and have relatively low cost associated with printing. If fact, you many want to compare how much it costs you to print it with your printer.

Flyers can be put in local business establishments, your office, your building (entry way table or elevators). If you have the manpower or want to do the "leg work" yourself, they can also be distributed on street corners, subways, and under windshield wipers.

I have used flyers in the following ways:

Remind client's or prospects that we offer Gift Certificates during the Thanksgiving and Christmas holidays as well as Valentine's Day, Mother's Day and Father's Day

Offer a Valentine's Day Special

Offer Specials-of-the-Month

Offer Monday Massage - $10 off on Mondays. Do you have a day that is slow? Maybe you haven't worked that day in the past and want to build your business on that day. If so, offer a discount until you build your clientele for that day.

Referral Incentives

Some clients will talk about you and your business without anything in return. But to keep everyone happy and talking, offer your clients referral incentives.

In my research, I have seen some therapists who offer "buy 1, get 1 free". I think that this is too much of a discount (If you charge $70 per hour, it costs you $70 to get that client, which is pretty steep). I do recommend offering a referral program for your existing clients.

When your existing clients send you a referral, send them a post card offering for 10% discount on their next service (You can also e-mail this). Always give an expiration date because it will prompt that client to make an appointment quickly. I usually give them a month and a half after the referral. It only costs you $7 to get this client at the $70 per hour fee. This is the approach I have taken in the past, and it has worked well for me.

You can also give the referred client a percentage or a dollar amount off. I don't do this because I take care of them with a coupon for $5 off for filling out the Client Survey Form (See Appendix A for example).

According to statistics, it cost one-fifth as much to keep an old customer as it does to earn a new one. So treat them with love, loyalty, devotion, consideration and professionalism so that you can keep them. Thirty-four percent of MassageWorks clients, not including those clients who have been given gift certificates, have been referred.

Marketing Alliances

Marketing Alliances, also called fusion marketing, can be one of the most rewarding, inexpensive, underused and effective marketing methods you can use.

There are two types of Marketing Alliances that I will talk to you about. One is basically free, and the other may involve a commission.

First, let's discuss the free way. You do this by putting your brochures, business cards or signs in another business in exchange for (but not always) putting their information in yours. Naturally, this works best if the two businesses are in some way complementary.

You may want to code your brochures or business cards so that you know which location produced the new business.

I have seen the idea of Marketing Alliances work in several ways. You can:

Share printing costs or create joint ads.

Provide an incentive by giving the other business a percentage of each sale when the customer shows the brochure picked up in their establishment.

Do group promotions.

Simply exchange each other's collateral material for the benefit of your clients. You may want to stop in periodically to refresh your supply of brochures and cards as well as get a new supply from them.

Here are some types of businesses you may want to create Marketing Alliances with:

Chiropractors
Acupuncturists
Yoga or Pilates Studios
Gyms
OB/GYN Doctors (if you do pregnancy and/or infant massage)
Speech Therapists
Pediatricians (if you do infant massage)
Private Preschools
Wedding Planners
Travel Agents
Real Estate Agents
Podiatrists
Orthopedic Surgeons
Psychotherapists
Psychologists

My Experience with Free Marketing Alliances

I have not used this method to it's full advantage purely because I have been so busy with clients I have not had the time to cultivate it.

I have two marketing alliances. One is my OB/GYN and one is my chiropractor. With my OB/GYN, I provide my brochure and a coupon for 15% off their first visit, which he puts into his "New Mother" packets. This is a "win-win" partnership because I get clients and my doctor is providing his patients with a value-added service.

My marketing alliance with my chiropractor is a mutual exchange of business cards. This is also a "win-win" partnership because I have someone to refer my clients to should they need a chiropractor and vice versa.

My calculations for this category are lumped in with my word-of-mouth in Chapter 4.

My Experience with Paid Marketing Alliances

I have two paid marketing alliances: SpaWish and Simply Certificates.

When I was doing my research for my Web site, I did a search on "Spas". A company called SpaWish kept coming up. I was curious.

I visited their Web site and noticed that someone could purchase a gift certificate for another person who didn't necessarily have to live in the same state. After digging a little deeper, I realized that the recipient of a SpaWish Gift Certificate would also get a booklet with over 1000 participating businesses where they could "spend" the gift certificate. For example, if I was a SpaWish gift certificate recipient, I would simply look in the booklet under "Virginia" and see the available locations for my state.

This concept was fascinating, and I wanted to know how I could be a participating location. There was a "contact us" link, so I emailed them to ask them the requirements. Since I offered massage therapy as well as spa treatments I was qualified. The cost is $96 per year to be linked on their Web site, plus 15% of the face value of the gift certificate. Here are my results from SpaWish Gift Certificates:

SpaWish

Percentage of Clients:	13%
Percentage of Income:	11%
Percentage of Advertising:	13.1%
Cost Per Client:	$12.28

SpaWish is the third most expensive advertising that I do. It is also 4th in the number of clients and 5th in the amount of income it produces. Twelve people from this group have referred one or more people with one referring seven.

Some people have seen my link on the SpaWish Web site, but have called me directly to order gift certificates so the 15% commission is eliminated. One person even heard about SpaWish on the Howard Stern radio show, checked the SpaWish Web site and then called me directly.

Almost 22% of SpaWish clients are repeats with my average income per client $170.61.

Would I do this one again? Definitely!

Simply Certificates

Simply Certificates is a national chain that rents kiosk space in malls and offers gift certificates from local merchants. You can find out more about them at www.simplycertificates.com.

In November 2002 a sales person from Simply Certificates approached me about becoming a provider. They are located in Tysons II Mall in McLean, Virginia.

There were no up front costs involved as with SpaWish, but a percentage (20%) of the face value is charged. Since it didn't cost anything until I got a client, I saw not reason not to. You just provide them with your brochures or other marketing literature.

Percentage of Clients:	>1%
Percentage of Income:	>1%
Percentage of Advertising:	>1%
Cost Per Client:	$6.66

These numbers may seem low, but you have to remember that it has only been a few months and I have never supplied them with any more brochures since he was first at my office. You're right. I need to follow-up.

I have gotten a total of nine clients from Simply Certificates. Two have been referrals. Two have seen my name at the Simply Certificate kiosk but called me directly. This man called me less than a week after I signed on as a participating merchant. I had almost forgotten that I had done it.

Would I do this one again? Of course! The cost per client is relatively low and I don't have to pay for a client until I get the client so there is no uncertainty if my advertising will work.

Gift Certificates

Offering gift certificates plants ideas in the minds of your prospects and in the minds of their friends. To offer gift certificates:

Print up signs that say, "Ask about our gift certificates" or "Gift Certificates Available". I did this using Word and printed it on a high quality paper, framing them and placing them strategically throughout the premises. You can change the paper with the seasons.

Put the name of your company and logo at the top. Leave room for the dollar amount, the recipient and giver's names and an expiration date.

If you are going to create gift certificates in-house, make sure you use fine quality heavy paper stock.

My Experience with Gift Certificates

I have sold 314 gift certificates in the past two and a half years with an average price of $83.25 representing 13% of total income.

Since I did the layout and design myself and I have them printed at Kinkos for approximately $.50 each, I'd say that gift certificates are well worth my time.

Remember the Expiration Date

Occasionally, gift certificate recipients ask me, if I will honor a gift certificate that has expired. Almost always, my answer is "no." I say almost always. A couple of times I have relented and said "yes" because the person called about a week before it was going to expire (this one happened the be December 31st) and with the holiday and vacations and reduced staff, we were not able to get the person in, so I extended if for a week. An extremely good client purchased the gift certificate another time, and I weighed the costs of losing that client. I also relented that time.

I don't like to extend gift certificates beyond the expiration for the following reasons:

> Adults should accept the fact that a year is a year.
> It is extra work to keep that liability on the books indefinitely.
> Few gift certificate recipients become repeat clients especially if they have never had a massage before.

So why knock yourself out? Recipients of gift certificates probably received them because they can't afford or don't see the value in massage. Six percent of gift certificate recipients have become repeats, and some repeated because they received multiple gift certificates.

Industry standard is that 50% of all gift certificates go unused. My statistics are lower, at around 10%.

So what happens to the money from the expired gift certificates? You may want to look at it as free money, or you can do what I do. I make up new certificates and donate them to charities for awards or raffles.

Donate Your Gift Certificates to Charities

I have donated 32 gift certificates to charities over the past three years. Usually, I am asked to donate by clients for the various charities they support, but occasionally I get outside solicitations.

I have recently begun donating two gift certificates a month to Hospice of Northern Virginia to be given to their staff of nurses and social workers who do such a wonderful job caring for terminally ill patients. I did this because Elaine, a friend and client, had died the previous March from lung cancer. When there was no hope for recovery, she was sent home for the remainder of her time here and she had Hospice care. I continued to massage her every other day while she was at home, and I was able to see the care that she was receiving. As it was approaching the one-year anniversary of her death, I was reminded of what good care she received, and I wanted to give back. So I contacted the human resources director of Hospice of Northern Virginia, told her what I wanted to do and I have been doing it ever since. The first two recipients were the nurse and social worker who cared directly for Elaine.

If you have the opportunity, I would recommend that you donate gift certificates as well. Why? There are probably numerous reasons, but here are four:

I am creating goodwill with my clients.
I am helping a charity raise money for its cause.
I am giving back to the community.
I am receiving a tax-deductible contribution. This is not meant to be tax advice, so be sure to check with your tax advisor before taking the deduction.

Chapter 6

Networking

Jeffrey Gitomer, author of *The Sales Bible* says, "More than 50% of sales are made because of friendship." People prefer to do business with people they know, like and trust.

What is networking? It is not moving through a room, handing out lots of cards, returning to your office and waiting for the phone to ring. Networking is meeting people and building long-term relationships.

Networking can be a powerful marketing tool if you use it to its fullest advantage. I know many business owners who have secured all their business by networking at various social clubs, country clubs, service clubs, professional clubs, health clubs, trade associations, and other organizations. This certainly is an option depending on the goals of your business and how fast you want to grow.

Here is where those business cards come in handy. Remember I said that one of the "Don'ts" is forget to have them with you at all times.

If you are at an organized networking function of one of the groups you belong to, have plenty of cards with you. I learned the following from one of my colleagues: If you are a woman, wear a suit that has a pocket, and don't carry a handbag (They are cumbersome and get in the way especially when you are shaking hands). Have your cards in one pocket and put the business cards you collect in the other pocket. Immediately after meeting a person make notes about him or her on the back of the card (meeting place and date, occupation, and any problems mentioned). The next day, send a follow-up letter with any requested information, summarize your conversation and mention where you met. Offer ways that you might be able to help.

Use the computer to network. Use chat rooms, bulletin boards, and other ways to talk with people. Some good networking groups to join are:

local AMTA chapter

Chamber of Commerce

BNI (Business Networking International). You can find out more about this organization at www.bni.com.

Women's or men's networking groups

Club and association memberships (i.e. Junior League, Kiwanas)

You can also find networking events in your local newspaper's business section or at www.networkinggroups.com.

There are many of the benefits of joining networking groups. Here are a few:

Meet potential prospects;

Members could refer clients;

Find like-minded suppliers, and

Build personal as well as professional relationships.

To do networking properly and get the most out of the experience, here are some rules to follow:

Rule #1: Give people a clear idea of what you do

Usually when you are introducing yourself in a group setting, you have about one minute to tell everyone who you are and what you do. You should have a rehearsed 60-second introduction as well as a 10-second one. Why rehearsed? Because then you know exactly what you are going to say and are not stammering for words or making it too lengthy.

The following information for the 60-second and 10-second introductions was derived from the information I learned in several networking seminars as well as my time as a member of BNI.

Anatomy of a 60-Second Introduction

Part 1: Introduction (18 seconds)

You'll give your name, position, company name, and an overview of products and/or services.

Hi, my name is Linda Steele and I am the owner of MassageWorks. We provide massage therapy, facials, body treatments, nail care and health-related classes to the general public.

Part 2: Tell a Story (20 seconds)

What makes you different from you competition? Share a specific, recent story that exemplifies what makes you different.

This past week I had an appointment with Eric, a client I have been working with every week for about three months. He had surgery on this rotator cuff as a result of a tear from playing tennis. He had just been to his orthopedic surgeon and the doctor was pleased with his progress. Originally Eric was told that he would only regain about 70-75% of his range of motion. But Eric already had back 95%.

Part 3: Ask for the Business (10 seconds)

A good referral for me is (be very specific)….

A good referral for me this week would be someone like Eric who has just had surgery and either wants to work with a massage therapist in conjunction with physical therapy or is finished with physical therapy, but hasn't gained back as much range of motion as expected.

Part 4: Call to Action (5 seconds)

"So if you see/hear/know of _____ please give him/her my card."

So if you know of anyone who has had surgery and is still suffering from pain or lack of movement, please give them my card.

Part 5: Tag Line (7 seconds)

A tag line, also called a memory hook, is something entertaining or clever so that people will remember you. After your tag line, conclude with your name and company.

If you want to take care of your body so your body can take care of you, remember massage works. My name is Linda Steele from MassageWorks. Thank you.

Anatomy of 10-Second Introduction

You should also have a shorter version prepared for when you meet someone in an elevator or other occasions where you are not given a minute to speak. The components of a 10-second introduction are as follows:

Greeting
Name and Company Name
What You Do
Tag Line

Now here is your chance to create your own 60-second and 10-second introductions.

60-Second Introduction

Part 1: Introduction (18 seconds)

_____

_____

_____

_____

Part 2: Tell a Story (20 seconds)

_____

_____

_____

_____

Part 3: Ask for the Business (10 seconds)

_____

_____

_____

_____

Part 4: Call to Action (5 seconds)

_____

_____

_____

_____

Part 5: Tag Line (7 seconds)

_____

_____

_____

_____

10-second Introduction

Greeting
Name and Company Name

_____

What You Do

_____

Tag Line

_____

Rule #2: Take plenty of cards (everywhere)

Carry more cards than you need. Keep cards in your wallet, briefcase or pockets as well as in your car.

Rule #3: Give people a good impression

Components of a good impression are your physical appearance and the affective energy you emit. You should dress for specific event, as people are more comfortable with their own kind. This energy refers to your attitude. It should be positive, and you should show enthusiasm.

Rule #4: Take the initiative

To start a conversation: Say something like "Hi (Welcome or Good morning), my name is Linda Steele".

To maintain a conversation: Ask open-ended questions such as "Where else do you network? Who else do you know here? Who else here should I talk to? This gives you control as well as relieving the other person from having to think of what to say. It also shows an interest in the information the other person has.

To end a conversation: Focus on the other person. "It was great to meet you. I'll let you go now so you can get around to meet other people."

Rule #5: Give people your full attention

Elements of dynamic listening:
Eye contact. Don't stare, but look at them.
Body posture. Lean slightly toward the person you are having a conversation with and stand shoulder to shoulder at an angle.
Use facial expressions. Mirror the person you are talking to.
Exercise restraint. Pause a few seconds after they have stopped talking to make sure they were not just thinking of how to say their next thought.
Ask questions. Questions show interest.
Paraphrase. You might say something like this. "If I understand you correctly, you..." and paraphrase what they just said. This helps clarify.
Empathize.

Rule #6. Take other people's cards

You have control.
Take notes because you won't remember them 72 hours later.
Note their real name.
Transfer the information to a contact management system.

Rule #7: Give people a hand

There is an old saying, "you reap what you sow." By giving people help with what they need, you will be creating a vacuum that allows you to receive. Here are some ways to serve:
Give referrals
Ways to serve your organization
-       Be on a committee
-       Help people find business
-       Explain purpose of organization
-       Promote organization
-       Find employees
-       Understand goals
-       Host networking events
-       Volunteer

Rule #8: Take the time to follow up

Here are some strategies:

> Send a thank-you letter or e-mail
> Make a phone call
> Send an article you think may be of interest
> Give notebook or gag bags with promotional information
> Send either your newsletter or one you think might be of
interest
> Give them a referral

My Experience with Networking Groups

I joined two networking groups: BNI and the Fairfax County Chamber of Commerce, but I kept my memberships active for only one year. I found that I was too busy to go to any of the events the Chamber sponsored and the time commitment for BNI was too great. If I were only going to grow my business by "free" advertising, I would join these networking groups again. Don't get me wrong, I think that these groups provide powerful contacts, but they have to be cultivated. Since I didn't have time to go to the events because of how busy I was at work, I was just wasting my money.

BNI

Percentage of Clients:	2.7%
Percentage of Income:	2.2%
Percentage of Advertising:	2.6%
Cost Per Client:	$11.81

Fairfax County Chamber of Commerce

Percentage of Clients:	>1%
Percentage of Income:	>1%
Percentage of Advertising:	2.6%
Cost Per Client:	$91.25

Chapter 7

Now That You Got Them, Don't Lose Them

Suzy Orman entitled her book *You've Earned It, Don't Lose It*. Even though it is about saving for retirement, the statement applies here as well. You have paid a certain amount of money to get a particular client in the door; do you want to lose him? I don't think so.

Rebooking Clients

Don't overlook rebooking your clients as a powerful marketing method. It is much easier for you and your client to get on your schedule for their next massage right after they have had one, especially if it is a good one.

As you start to get busier, you are going to want to make sure that your good clients are already booked when they want to see you. You never want to be completely booked when they call.

I have a very good client who gets a 90-minute massage every other week. At the beginning, he didn't want to commit to scheduling the next one because he didn't know his schedule. A couple of times he called and I had no openings. Because he was a good client, I went out of my way to fit him in somewhere by coming in early or staying late. I didn't want him to keep getting discouraged by not being able to get in and eventually go somewhere else. The next time he was in, I mentioned that I want to make sure he gets the time that he wants and suggested we schedule him now. If he needs to change it later, he can, but at least he has a reserved spot.

How do you get a first-timer to rebook? I explain the importance of regular massage and ask if they would like to get on the schedule for next time. Then I wait for the response. If the question is "How often should I get a massage?" I say that some get a massage once a week, some twice a week and some once a month. Depending on your pocketbook and your stress level, once a month is a good start to keep you relaxed and your muscles loose. Then I wait for the response. There is an old saying in sales, "He who talks first, loses." So by saying something else you give the client a way out. Some people think that this may be misleading, but my view is that you are providing a valuable needed service to your client and you want your calendar full.

Keeping In Touch

If you don't stay in touch with your clients, someone else will. According to statistics, 80 percent of business is lost due to apathy after the sale.

Follow-up Customer Survey

This should go out a day or two after a new client's first appointment. I send a cover letter, the survey, a $5 coupon, and a self-addressed stamped envelope. The $5 off coupon is for their next visit and usually expires 30-45 days after the mailing goes out. The idea is to thank them for their visit, get feedback about their impression of MassageWorks and any improvements they would suggest, and keep us in the forefront of their minds to schedule another massage if they didn't schedule one at the time of their appointment. See Appendix A for a sample of the letter, survey and $5 off coupon.

Forty percent of our follow-up customer surveys have been returned. The response rate for direct mail according to most marketing textbooks, is 1-2%. So to get a 40% return is phenomenal.

Why do I think I got so many returned surveys? Well, it certainly wasn't the $5 off coupon since only 35% of the people returning a survey have used the coupon. I don't think that it was because they didn't come back as clients they just may have forgot their coupon or it expired (Remember the coupons are good for 30-45 days assuming that everyone should have a massage once a month) before they came back.

I think the reason for my success is that people are surprised and pleased that they were asked for their opinion. As a consumer, think how many times you have received a survey for something you bought. I bet you can count them on one hand maybe two. People like to be asked what they think and give suggestions on ways a service could be improved. Since, the surveys are anonymous, it allows people to freely express their opinions.

Here are some comments from the surveys as well as how we handled the comment.

Under "Suggested Improvements"

"Candles and music in the lobby."

I added music in the waiting room, but I decided against the candles for two reasons: They couldn't be watched at all times when we are in session, and it is hard to find unscented candles that respect people's sensitivities to fragrances.

"I know your facilities are limited, but it would have been nice to soak in a hot tub or relax in a sauna to relax prior to the massage. I felt rushed."

In response to this, we added a foot massager in the waiting area where clients sit while filling out their paperwork."

"Make the room darker – perhaps black curtains."

In my treatment room, I have always had black curtains on the windows. The other two treatment rooms are multi-use so I haven't covered the windows. In response to this, we have eye pillows for the client's who wish to use them when they are supine.

"Let clients know there is paperwork to be filled out so it does not take time from their sessions to complete it. Tell them to come in 15 minutes early for the first appointment."

We do ask the clients to come in 15 minutes early and even repeat it several times during the conversation. However, they don't always show up early. When possible we still give them their full time. In response to this we have started asking people who don't show up 15 minutes early if they had trouble finding us. This usually jogs their memory that they were supposed to be there before their appointment time.

"Have a nice aromatherapy scent in the room or under the massage table."

Because many people have allergies and sensitivities to smells, we decided not to have scented candles burning all the time in the treatment room, but we can use scented candles or use essential oils with the massage if requested.

"Price is a little higher than many places – could offer some discount packages for multiple visits".

The last time I checked in my area, my price was right in line with everyone else. So I am not sure where they are getting their massage.

"More information over phone – would have schedule 90-minutes if I had known it was available."

I am not really sure what happened with this one. All I can say is that I do tell people that we have times for massages from 30 minutes to 2 hours and give the various prices for each. I have trained my staff to do the same.

"Treatment was customized for most clients rather than me – would have preferred face up first."

Since this client signed her name I know that it was a HotStone massage she received. The HotStone massage protocol I am trained in specifies that you start the client prone for ease in stone placement, etc. For regular massages, however, I usually talk over with the clients what is going on that day and make a decision whether to start them prone or supine. I do tend to want to work on the client's back first in a full body, but I ask the client if there is a preference.

"Room was a little cool."

We try to keep the facilities at 72 degrees in the summer and 75 degrees in the winter so that we as therapists are comfortable working. In response to the temperature issue, when a client is there for the first time, we explain that the table warmer is on full and that if they are too hot let us know and we can turn it down. If they are cold, we can provide another blanket. So as people return they know that they can speak up about the temperature. We also know them as clients and know if they run hot we can turn the table warmer off before they get there.

"Heavily scented candles by entrance could cause problems for people with respiratory ailments."

The "heavily scented candles" this client is speaking of are actually soaps with essential oils. I do realize that a lot more people have allergies and other sensitivities, so in response to this, we have moved the soaps so that they are a little more out of the way and not right next to people as they are filling out the intake form.

"Lower/dim lights in lobby common areas at night so to keep that relaxed feeling after massage in evening."

In response to this suggestion, for evening massage we now turn off the overhead lights in the waiting area and just leave a low-level light on. I must admit, the fluorescent lights were a bit too bright, and the brightness was a shock after just coming out of a dark room and being very relaxed. It was something I knew but didn't pay much attention to because we don't do many evening appointments.

"Paint and decorate walls to give less office aura; move computer out of massage room; perhaps some sound proofing to muffle traffic noise."

Some things cannot be changed. I am limited by what I can do to the office space by my landlord, who specified the color of paint I can have. Sound proofing the walls is also not possible without changing the configuration of the office suite, something I would have to have approved by the landlord. I did however move the computer out of my treatment room and into the waiting room.

"Outside environment noisy (traffic, construction)". "Maybe not have the massage room near a window where you can hear the traffic." "Try to jazz up the outside of the office a little – bad building, but the inside was nice." "Needs to be located in a less dumpy building. However, your facilities are fine. Building looks dirty."

The traffic I can't do anything about until I move locations and since it doesn't bother everyone it is something that will just have to be for right now. This survey was written in the beginning when our building was going through a massive renovation. It did look very shabby when I moved in. The new owner just bought the building two months previous and was planning a major renovation. This is one of the reasons I moved there. For about a year we had to put up with the construction noise. It really had very little effect on my business.

If someone was new to the business, I would let him or her know when they were scheduling their appointment that our building was under construction. I found that most people didn't even hear the noise and quite a few still fell asleep during the massage.

Some of the comments below I received at the same time that I received surveys with the suggestions above. People perceive things differently, so don't become all upset about a suggestion if it implies a negative experience. I usually view the area of suggestion with the outsider's eye and ask myself the following questions: (1) Is this really a problem for everyone? (2) How many times have I seen this suggestion? (3) Can I do anything about this? (4) Is it cost-effective to make the change? (5) Does my lease allow me to make these changes?

Here are some comments that clients put under "Additional Comments."

"I would definitely return again. This survey is a nice touch, information for you, but also a good tool for repeat business. I am very pro women-owned business, so I have already spread the word to my friends about MassageWorks."

"My massage was perfect. I had gone on a 20-mile run prior to it. I was not sore at all the next day."

"Very nice session and great environment! Thank you."

"I'm interested in receiving ear candling; you are the only place I know that offers it!"

"I called several massage places. I was most impressed with your Web site, so I chose to come to you. Also, you are very conveniently located. Thanks!"

"Just had a massage a week earlier from someone else (different place) and was disappointed. Kate, on the other hand, did great, especially for a new person. She really listened to what I wanted. She'll be even better with experience, I expect."

"She really concentrated where I needed work rather than just going through a routine like so many other massages I have had."

"Loved the warmed massage table!"

"I enjoyed MassageWorks. The office is quite relaxing – great for massage. Thank you."

"A very personal and warm atmosphere. Thanks so much for the experience."

"No suggestions for MassageWorks. Only wish that their building was not under construction. Best massage I've ever received."

"I will be back. I liked the fact that you provide full service. I want to try your manicures and pedicures."

"Great job of returning calls – prompt and very polite. A key selling point. Look forward to my next one."

"The office is very professional, which immediately put me at ease the first time I visited. Kathy did a magnificent job during my massage. She got rid of my problems and I was not sore the next day! The young man who was at the front desk is very friendly (and cute!!) and helpful. He basically sold me on the ear candling, which I otherwise wouldn't have asked about. I'll definitely be back, and I'll spread the word!"

"Keep up the good work. Excellent ways to keep clients interested with letter and coupons."

"I get the email newsletter which I find interesting to read."

Birthday card

I send my clients a birthday card during their birth month. I used to send an actual card to everyone, but mailing costs as the client base grew got to be expensive, so now I send an e-birthday card. If I don't have an email address for a customer, then I will send an actual card if they are regulars.

I send them all out at the beginning of the month and they expire at the end of the month. I give my really good clients (i.e. regulars) a 25% discount, and all others $10 off.

Newsletters and E-Newsletters

Newsletters are extremely flexible and inexpensive to produce if you decide to do it yourself with desktop-publishing.

Newsletters can also establish you as an authority as it proves your expertise. Many people take anything in print as the truth. That is why the media is so powerful. People remember 68% of what they read. It makes a great direct mail piece, a perfect way to keep your name in front of prospects and clients. It helps you strengthen your bond with your customers and increases their level of confidence.

The best newsletters are short, four to eight pages maximum. Give a lot of information, but in short paragraphs. Use short sentences. Use short words. Tell people news. Have several people write the newsletter since everyone has a different style. Mail or e-mail it monthly if you can, otherwise as often as possible.

For an example of MassageWorks E-Newsletter see Appendix A.

Other Ideas for Keeping in Touch

A holiday card. I send a holiday card to my client base and include a coupon for a discount to be used the next year. Until this past year, I sent cards to the whole client base excluding those who only purchased gift certificates and those from out-of-town. With the rising client base and costs associated with buying cards and postage, I eliminated one-timers and those who haven't been in a while.

My coupon is valid for January and February. I picked the two full months because it gives people time to recuperate from excessive spending they may have done during the holidays. This time is usually slower for most massage practices, however, you may only want to give one month.

I actually make these discounts cards using the ready-made business cards you can purchase at any office supply store. It reads as follows:

Thank you for your continued support. This
entitles you to 10% off your next visit.
Offer good January 1 – February 28, 2003.
MassageWorks, Inc.
450 W. Broad St., Suite 412
Falls Church, VA 22043
(703) 536-7200

A contest. You could hold a Mother's Day or Father's Day contest.

An anniversary card. Send a card to your client on the anniversary date of when they started seeing you.

A research questionnaire. Want to improve in the level of service you give or find out what clients want, send them a questionnaire and ask.

Chapter 8

Get Out There and Talk

Lectures

Presenting talks about your business can do wonders to establish yourself as an authority. These usually are given free of charge or for a small fee to cover expenses.

You can offer to give your services as a speaker at local clubs and service organizations. You may also want to check major corporations in your area who overtly support their employee's mental and physical health. Contact the human resources department and ask if the company would be interested in your program about the health benefits of massage, stress reduction techniques or other specialties. Your strongest sales pitch is the potential reduction in days lost from work when employees are healthier.

When thinking about embarking on the lecture circuit, remember these points:

Lecture only if you are a dynamic speaker. If you are not, you and your topic will be uninteresting. Do you remember your favorite teacher in school? You probably do. You may not remember anything about the subject. What made them your favorite teacher? It was probably that they were the most enthusiastic and energetic when talking about the subject.

If you fear that you are a boring speaker or maybe are afraid of pubic speaking, it may show in your delivery, and you may turn people off. If you know you aren't a dynamic speaker, there's hope and help. You may want to check out Toastmaster's or a voice coach (see Resource Guide).

I highly recommend using visual aids (i.e. transparencies, slides, products, or demonstrations) whenever possible. Why? Because most people process information through different senses and are not exclusively auditory learners so having something to look at helps in understanding. A side note: If you can work in visual, auditory and kinesthetic learning, people will remember more because three senses are engaged. If you need to use your own products or services, that's fine, but make sure you are only using them for illustration, not selling them.

If you use your lecture as a forum to sell your services, it may be perceived as giving a "free" lecture under false pretenses, and it will probably be resented.

Always think about the people in your audience and what you can give them. Knock yourself out by giving important information and/or advancement in the massage industry.

While you are not there specifically to sell your services, there will likely be someone who needs your service and may want to contact you. So speak your company's name as well as show contact information so that people can reach you. You may even want to provide some sort of coupon for a free service or discount.

I presented a lecture on hand maintenance to a Web development company whose employees use the computer 95% of the day. During the lecture, I talked about repetitive stress injuries and showed them exercises and stretches for the hands, arms and neck. I gave them a coupon for 15% off their first visit with my handouts.

Another time, I was asked to give a lecture on essential oils to Freddie Mac in McLean, Virginia. I demonstrated some of the oils, provided handouts and gave my 15% off coupons.

Seminars and Workshops

Offer presentations on topics you know well. If you screened carefully, you could even hire people to teach the classes. This would not only add additional income to your bottom line from the fees for the seminars or workshops, but also get your name out there to more workshop attendees who may not be familiar with your services.

What topics would work well?

The possible topics are endless, but here are some samples. I hope they inspire you with more ideas.

> Chakras and/or Pendulums
> Ergonomic Workplace
> Essential Oils
> Feng Shui
> Flexibility and Stretching
> Infant massage
> Massage for Couples Series:

> (1) Neck, Shoulders and Back;
> (2) Scalp and Face; and
> (3) Reflexology for the Feet

Nutrition
Reiki
Self Care
Self-help in some particular area
Stress Management

What to charge

When deciding what to charge, you should take into consideration the length of the seminar or workshop (both in hours and days), the amount of expertise necessary, and what the competition is charging for similar seminars or workshops.

With the exception of my Ergonomic Workplace seminar, Infant Massage workshop, Reiki classes and the Massage for Couples workshops, my seminars and workshops have usually been 2-3 hours long with a typical charge of $25-35.

Trade Shows and Health Fairs

Trade shows are put on by an organization and tailored to a group or an industry. The organizer will usually provide booth space for a fee. While my experience with trade shows is limited in the massage arena, in my previous career, I used to manage and attend quite a few per year. So I speak from experience that they can be wonderful opportunities to add names of prospective clients to your mailing list and give you added exposure. Health fairs are basically trade shows that are customized for the health industry. They can be organized by large or small companies that are employee-friendly and health-conscious.

There are several things that will increase the traffic flow to your booth and enhance the potential success of your event. They are:

Send an e-mail or post card to your client base, telling them you will be at this particular trade show or health fair.

If you have adequate notice of the event, make sure you include it in your monthly newsletters or e-newsletters.

Have someone posted at the entrance or other strategic locations, handing out postcards directing people to your display.

Have a colorful, attractive presentation area.

Advertise in the event brochure if the cost is not too high and is in your marketing budget.

Host a drawing for a free massage. Have people enter simply by dropping their business card into a bowl or filling out a card. These names should be added to your mailing list. Also, send them a special offer with your marketing material within 30 days.

You can find trade shows and health fairs by contacting your local Chamber of Commerce or looking in alternative health newspapers publications.

My Experience with Trade Shows

Percentage of Clients:	>1%
Percentage of Income:	>1%
Percentage of Advertising:	1.3%
Cost Per Client:	$87.50

I have only done one trade show (Festival of Lights, Falls Church, Virginia) since I have been in business. This is not because I don't think that it was worth it; I do. It all has come down to timing of the events and my schedule.

While my numbers may look low as only two clients resulted from this venue, other factors need to be considered. First, it has the highest income per client of all of the marketing methods used, coming in at $929.87 per client. In addition, I also provided seated massage as well as selling retail items at the event pulling in over $1000 for the day.

Do I think I could have improved my results? Absolutely. How? Mailing literature and discount coupons to those entering the drawing even though I gave information to all those who stopped by. I think it is important to mail the information because it reminds them of who you are and they may have been inundated with information that day that they will never look at again.

My Experience with Health Fairs

I have done a few health fairs, all for large corporations. Since I didn't pay a fee for the booth, I have included their statistics in free advertising.

I have not done any health fairs recently, but I would if my schedule permitted.

I'd make the same improvements I stated above.

Chapter 9

Public Relations and Publicity

I first wrote this chapter as I was approaching my two-year anniversary. It took me a year to write that version of the book, ending it with writing my own press releases celebrating our 2nd anniversary with an open house featuring free postural analysis screenings. Since that time I have changed this chapter slightly adding some advice from Steve Winter who is a co-owner of Brotman, Winter, Fried Communications, a public relations firm in Falls Church (For more information, see Resource Guide).

So what is public relations? According to Steve, it is "media exposure that can reach out to prospective clients, establishing credibility through awareness and that doesn't cost you anything."

A former public relations consultant once said that what is believed about an organization can be more important than what is true about an organization! With this in mind, a properly utilized public relations plan can reinforce advertising, expand your message reach, establish or add credibility, generate excitement and support, tell the whole story, reach distinct and special audiences, and create public acceptance.

Readers tend to put more trust in printed news than in advertising therefore publicity can be one of your most cost-effective marketing tools.

In the following paragraphs are steps you might use if you were to handle your own public relations effort. Should going it alone sound too daunting and your budget allows, you may want to seek professional help. Steve Winter has graciously given me some advice and tips to pass along to you on how to find a good firm and the fee you might expect to pay.

Going It Alone

I didn't need a professional public relations effort prior to my two-year anniversary as I had more clients than I could handle most of the time, but you may decide to use PR right from the beginning.

I decided to go it alone because in my previous career I handled public relations for the entire company.

While I do not think it is hard running your own PR campaign, it does, take some effort. I have outlined five steps you can use to build your own plan.

Step 1: Planning for Public Relations

Your first project will be to get acquainted with the people in charge of selecting stories to be covered. Where do you find media contacts? Check your local library and look up two sources Bacon's Publicity Checker and Working Press of the Nation (see the Resource Guide for further information).

If this task seems too large, or if you want to stay in your immediate area, find the name of the business editor or health editor of your local newspaper(s). Contact the publication directly to verify the name and spelling. Few things are more flattering than having one's name spelled correctly, and few things scream "bulk mailing" more than a misspelled name. Mail I get with my name misspelled is thrown into the trash, and yours probably is too. When you have verified information, send your press release to that person.

Step 2: A Newsworthy Story

Newspaper and magazine publishers want fascinating news because this helps them sell their publications. You want exposure because it helps you sell your services. The two can mesh if you have a newsworthy story they can feature.

A good thing to do is to watch the local news and read the local papers to see what kind of stories they are featuring and keep a journal for future reference. The first year I decided to have the Valentine's Day couples massage (more about this in Chapter 10), I just happened to be watching ABCs Channel 7 evening news a day or two before Valentine's Day and Del Walters did a feature story on ways to make your Valentine feel special. Unfortunately, my Valentine's Couples massage special was not one of them.

The following are a few ideas to get you thinking:

Have you done seated massage at a charity event, a local or not-so local marathon, or a disaster site? After September 11, 2001 stories abounded about massage therapists lending their hands to help ease the tragic results near the World Trade Centers and the Pentagon.

Have you donated a gift certificate to a silent auction for a prominent local charity or for some other cause? After September 11, I donated a gift certificate to rescue workers helping at the Pentagon. I also regularly donate gift certificates to Hospice.

Are you having an open house?

Are you celebrating an anniversary?

Did you add a new service, product, or even a prominent local massage therapist to your staff?

Are you offering a special such as Valentine's Day couples massage?

Step 3: Send a press release

Your press release should answer the who? what? where? when? and why? and sometimes how?

There are six key elements in a press release. They are as follows:

Company information at top of the page: Name of company, address, phone number,

Contact information: Include contact person(s) and telephone number(s).

On the right side of page type on that same line, type "For Immediate Release" or "For Release on [a certain date]".

The headline. This is your who? and what? It grabs the attention of the reader and should be in all capitals and underlined.

Next comes the body of the press release. Important details should be in the lead paragraphs. Less important details should follow.

At the end, type "# # #" in the center of the page to indicate the end of the story.

See Appendix A for a sample of a press release.

Step 4: Follow-up

When dealing with press releases follow-up is important. Call the editor a day or two in advance of your event. Introduce yourself and ask if he or she received your press release. Invite the person to your event. The press may not attend or bring a camera crew. If you don't try, however, you can be assured coverage will be unlikely.

By following up, you get your name in front the editor again, or maybe for the first time, as he or she might not have read your press release. It also gives you a chance to get to know each other. By your giving it this special attention and extending a personal invitation, the editor may decide to come to the event and bring a camera crew.

Step 5: Develop an on-going relationship with the media

People do business with people they know and like. Forming a relationship or friendship with someone in the press increases the odds that your press releases will become future feature stories.

Going With the Professionals

If you have read the previous section and decided the process is too involved for you, that's all right. That is why there are professionals. After all, where would we be if people decided to give themselves a massage or have a friend do it? Again, this section is the result of my interviewing Steve Winter of Brotman, Winter, Fried Communications.

How to find a PR firm?

Steve suggests that unless you are a large massage practice, your needs will be met by a small public relations company, preferably in your area. Since your primary customers will be coming from a 5-8 mile radius, it makes sense to go with a firm in the area who will be familiar with the media and the possible feature stories.

What can a PR firm do for you?

According to Steve, that at least, it can get you involved in community projects such as local fairs, and charity auctions and events. Given a longer lead-time, PR firms can get you radio and television spots as well as newspaper feature stories.

He says that this usually involves a 3-4 month commitment so that the public relations firm can find "quality angles" and "effectively pitch to local writers."

What should you expect to pay?

A public relations company can charge anywhere from $2,500 to $5,000 per month. If you have a limited budget, Steve suggests that you may want to find a company that will take payment on a partial or trade basis.

If this sounds like it might be out of your budget at the present time, some firms will take a single project or just write a press release for you.

Chapter 10
Special Events Marketing

Valentine's Day Couples Massages

About two weeks before Valentine's Day last year, the idea of having couples massage came to me. This would allow a couple to have massages in the same room. We had a room large enough to accommodate two massage tables, but I wasn't sure how it would go. I decided to give it a try. Since Valentine's Day fell on a Thursday, the special ran Thursday through Sunday. So I prepared a couple of flyers to put up in our building and on the Specials page of my Web site. Less that 24 hours later people were calling to book. We had 15 couples that weekend.

Our recent Valentines Day Couples Massage weekend had 11 couples. The numbers were lower, but the special lasted only three days (Friday through Sunday) and Sunday we had a snowstorm so we had to cancel that day. However, we were able to reschedule everyone the following weekend.

Mother's Day

For Mother's Day, I will usually have a special for a combo at a discounted price.

Here is the Mother's Day special for May 2002.

Special of the Month

Mother's Day is May 12th...Buy a gift certificate for that special mom for a massage and a facial, $125 (regularly $135). Gift certificates are good for one year but must be purchased by May 11th to get this special offer.

Father's Day

In the past for Father's Day, I have given a discount (usually 10%). While I do have some men who get facials and the other services we offer, they seem to be more massage types. So I tend to give the discounts either for a 90-minute massage or for the HotStone massage (either the hour or 90-minute).

Specials

I usually advertise specials as the "Special of the Month". They go in the e-Newsletter, on the Web site and in a display ad in the office. Specials of the month have been a selected service for a discount (either a dollar amount or percentage off). Other times I have done a combo (i.e. massage and facial) for a dollar discount.

Here is an example of the Special of the Month for April 2002:

Special of the Month

Ear Candling - Ear candling is used primarily for cleaning the ears and to promote a healthy atmosphere in the ears, sinus cavities and throat. The process can also regulate pressure, assist with post nasal drip, sinusitis, migraines, some forms of hearing loss, restoration of equilibrium, relieving tinnitus, vertigo and Meniere's Syndrome.

Regularly $75; Now $65.
(This offer expires 4/30/02 and cannot be combined with any other discount.)

Contests

I have held only one contest, Mother's Day contest of 2002. Here is the ad in the e-Newsletter detailing it.

Mother's Day Contest

Enter your mother or the mother of your children in MassageWorks Mother's Day Contest.
Simply write in 500 words or less why your mom (or mother of your children) is the best and deserves to be pampered. She will be treated to the "My Pick Me Up" package which includes a one-hour massage, a corrective facial and a pedicure on the morning of Saturday, May 11th.

Also in your entry, please include the following information:
Your mother's name, your name, your age, your address (also your mom's address if different from yours) and your telephone number. Entries must be received by May 1st.
Winner will be notified week of May 6th. Mail your entry to

Mother's Day Contest, MassageWorks, 450 W. Broad Street, Suite 412, Falls Church, VA 22046 or E-mail to linda@massageworksinc.com

All entries become the property of MassageWorks and can not be returned.

We had 30 entries. All of the entries were beautifully written and it was hard to choose which one to pick. So I put all of the entries into a bowl and drew the winner's name that way.

Here is how I announced the winner to the MassageWorks community in the next month's e-Newsletter

Mother's Day Contest

The results are in…

We had so many wonderful letters telling us why their mom was the best and deserved to be pampered. It was hard to pick, but the mother winning the "My Pick Me Up" package is Sarah Riley of Manassas.

There are many other ideas to hold contests. They are only limited by your imagination. Here are a few examples to get you going.

- Father's Day Contest
- Favorite Kid Contest
- Name your e-Newsletter
- Favorite Charity Contest (to which you will donate a gift certificate)

End of the School Year Massages

This could be offered to teachers as well as students. Consider giving a discount of $10 or 10% off.

Chapter 11

Print Ads

There are a variety of publications to choose from: alternative magazines, local newspapers, weekly or bi-weekly newspapers, and regional newspapers.

Sources say it takes about nine times seeing a particular ad before someone will actually perceive what is says and act on it. When thinking about using newspaper ads as a marketing method, you should think in terms of using them consistently at least bi-weekly if not weekly. Since you will want to run the ad repeatedly, I suggest you go with the biggest one you can afford.

Design

My suggestion to you would be to look through the various newspapers at the ads and see what grabs your attention. You might want to ask you friends and family to do this for you as well.

What are the elements common in the ads that catch your eye? One way to cut down the lead-time is to create an ad that will be noticed right away.

The components of an ad are:

theme or message stated in a simple, declarative sentence

headline, including the business name and a reader benefit

illustration showing the product or service

text which is used to explain the product or service and tell the reader what to do next and how to do it easily

trademark or logo of business with name, complete address, and phone number

Pricing

Pricing for newspaper ads is usually based on:

Circulation (how many readers do they have) of newspaper. A newspaper that has a larger circulation charges more because it reaches more people. For example, I checked two papers

	Circulation	Cost of 2 x 3 ad
Paper A	40,787	211.86
Paper B	32,484	183.60

Paper A has 20% more readers than Paper B and costs 13% more. That suggests Paper A may be the better investment.

Size of ad. Some papers have different size ads so ask for a media package. The ad size will usually be different from the actual measurement.

For example,

Available Ad Sizes	Mechanical Measurements
2 x 3	3 ¾" x 3"
2 x 6.5	3 ¾" x 6.5"
3 x 6.5 (quarter page)	5 ¾" x 6.5"
5 x 6.5 (half page)	9 5/8" x 6.5"
5 x 13 (full page)	9 5/8" x 13"

Frequency of ad placement. Most publications will quote you a price based on a one-time insertion. However, they will often offer you a discount for the commitment of multiple insertions. One newspaper I checked, was offering the following frequency discounts:

6 weeks	5%
8 weeks	10%
13 weeks	15%
26 weeks	20%
52 weeks	25%

So if I used Paper A (from above) where a one-time insertion was $211.86 and I committed to 26 weeks, I would receive 20% off the $211.86 or a $42.37 discount, but now I have obligated $4,406.74 ($169.49 x 26) of my advertising dollars.

Why I chose newspaper ads

I started my business in October which meant the Yellow Pages was not due out until late January. Newspapers became a way I could get my name out there quickly. I advertised in the following local papers:

Pathways, an alternative quarterly publication (I advertised quarterly).

Washington Woman, a monthly newspaper (I advertised monthly).

The Connection, a weekly newspaper (I advertised twice in this publication, once two weeks before my Grand Opening and then again the week before).

Sun Gazette, a weekly newspaper (I advertised bi-weekly).

Falls Church News Press, a weekly newspaper which serves the city in which my business is located (I advertised weekly).

My Experience with Newspaper Advertising

Percentage of Clients: 9.3%
Percentage of Income: 14%
Percentage of Advertising: 32%
Cost Per Client: $42

At the one-year mark the totals for newspaper advertising were 18%, 21%, 48% and $76.28 respectively.

The percentage of clients drawn from this source has decreased dramatically because the overall client base has increased significantly from other sources as has the percentage of income. The percentage of advertising has dropped 16%. While I have not advertised formally, my costs for Web site maintenance and my marketing alliances with SpaWish and Simply Certificates continue to cost me money.

In the next few pages, you will see how they stacked up individually.

Pathways Magazine

Percentage of Clients: 1%
Percentage of Income: 4.7%
Percentage of Advertising: 1.6%
Cost Per Client: $19

At the one-year mark the totals were 2.3%, 3.3%, 2% and $26 respectively.

The client base did grow here since I stopped advertising but insignificant in the overall total but it raked in another 25% from where it was. How can a client base grow when you are no longer advertising? The answer is referrals and newspaper ads may have a longer life that we think. Some people may see your ad but may not have time to react to it at the moment, so they keep it in their pile of papers until they get around to it or they really need a massage.

The cost did drop $7 per client because my client base grew but my cost remained the same.

Income from Pathways clients grew about 68% from where it was when I stopped advertising. From this, you can conclude that there are some very good repeat clients from this source. Actually, about 25% of the client base is responsible for 80% of the income. It actually does have the highest income to client ratio of all of the marketing methods I use at $924.27.

So would I use this method of advertising again? Definitely!

Washington Woman

Percentage of Clients:	2%
Percentage of Income:	2.3%
Percentage of Advertising:	4.7%
Cost Per Client:	$30

At the one-year mark the numbers were 3.3%, 2.8%, 5.7%, and $51 respectively.

Percentage of clients from this source increased 41% in the last two years. So again you can conclude that there are a lot of referrals from here or people hold on to back copies.

Income has increased 54% in the past two years. This has resulted from one person referring 31% of the clients who have, in turn, become regular clients. That person was actually responsible for 37% of the income.

Would I advertise with this paper again? Hindsight is 20/20. My return on investment was eight times what I spent. I think that this is pretty good return. I have developed a strong client from this source, who has brought me money in other ways as well. Although you can't guarantee you will get regular clients from any source, I would advertise in the Washington Woman again.

The Connection

Percentage of Clients:	>1%
Percentage of Income:	>1%
Percentage of Advertising:	3.8%
Cost Per Client:	$534

At the one year mark the numbers were >1%, >1%, 4.6%, and $534 respectively. There was only one client that resulted from the two times I advertised with this paper. She came pretty regularly but then moved out of the area.

If I had it to do again, I would not advertise with this paper. My reasons: 1) Each insertion cost well over $200 which is why I only advertised twice, 2) For consistency you would have to spend $4800 (bi-weekly at $200 for 12 months) which is quite expensive for the number of clients resulting from each newspaper (If you recall, all of the newspaper advertising I did resulted in only 9.3% of the clients).

Sun Gazette

Percentage of Clients:	1.6%
Percentage of Income:	2%
Percentage of Advertising:	18.9%
Cost Per Client:	$138

At the one-year mark, we were 3.5%, 2.6%, 23%, and $188 respectively.

Percentage of clients increased by 26% from the one-year mark as a result of one person referring seven people. Percentage of income increased 38% with one person responsible for 28% of the income.

I would not advertise in this paper again because of what it costs for me to be consistent. At about $187 per insertion (for a ¼-page ad) bi-weekly is almost $5000 per year. If I did advertise with this paper again, I would change the ad size to the smallest available. Because even with consistency the dollar amount spent would be more manageable. I might also try to get the best placement on the page if that is possible.

Percentage of Clients: 4.6%
Percentage of Income: 5.5%
Percentage of Advertising: 10.4%
Cost Per Client: $27

At the one-year mark we were 8.8%, 7.1%, 12.5%, and $41 respectively.

Income has grown 53% from this source since I stopped advertising. About four are responsible for 30% of the income from this source. Number of clients increased 34%, dropping the cost per client to $14. The client growth is mostly from referrals. Six people have referred one or two people and two people have referred three to four.

I would advertise with this newspaper again because it is local and serves where my business is located. It gave me an instant presence as some of the earliest clients came from the *Falls Church News Press*. It is also *good* business to *do* business within your community.

Chapter 12

Telephone Directory Ads

Depending on the area you live in, there could be many different telephone directories from the Yellow Pages to The One Book to many community directories. I advertised in the Yellow Pages because it is the oldest, best-known, and most of my friends and relatives use it.

Whichever directory you decide, this method gives you an opportunity to go head-to-head with the competition. Some guidelines about marketing in the telephone directory:

If you want quality referrals, make sure that you are listed under "Massage Therapists" and not "Massage" which to some people suggests illicit activities.

The people who seek out your ad tend to be honest prospects. Most people don't just browse the telephone directory for fun.

Be sure your ad provides loads of information. Don't waste valuable space or use unnecessary pictures. Give all of the benefits of doing business with you.

Get the largest ad you can afford since you are committed for 12 months at a time.

Give the job of designing your ad to a professional. That is part of the service provided when you contract with the Yellow Pages.

My Experience with Telephone Directory Advertising

Percentage of Clients: 15%
Percentage of Income: 14%
Percentage of Advertising: 12%
Cost Per Client: $9.35

At the one-year mark we were 17.8%, 10.7%, 14.5%, and $23.32 respectively.

If I had it to do over I would not have a Yellow Pages display ad but just the free listing I have now. My Yellow Pages advertising costs ranked fourth in the total number of dollars I spent. Since I stopped the display ad, my percentage of clients has increased almost 60%. Twenty-six percent of those clients have come from referrals the remaining from the free listing, a better return on your dollar.

Income has grown 71% since the one-year mark, allowing the cost per client to decrease by almost $14, but I have not reviewed the individual statistics from the one-year mark to know if most of the income growth has come from repeat business. Seven people in this group have spent over $700 each on our services.

Chapter 13

Web Sites

My experience differs with some other authors who have discounted the importance of Web sites. My experience shows and after you read this chapter, I think you will agree that Web sites are essential today. Many people are starting to look for companies on-line instead of going to the telephone book. Having a Web site gives credibility to your legitimacy and professionalism.

What to Look for in a Web site Development Company

There are three types development companies. The first is the traditional company that specializes in Web development. This type can be very expensive so here is what you will need to know.

Have a very good idea of what you want in your Web site. This company gives you a proposal for your plan, so every time you change your mind the price changes.

Find out about on-going support. Often times they charge a four-hour minimum. So if you save all of the changes you want made to make it worth the fee, your site can be out of date before changes are made.

This type of company usually charges $125-175 per page and hosting can be anywhere from $30-75 per month and may include one or two e-mail addresses.

The second is to build the Web site yourself or to have a relative or friend build it for you.

In you are going for this plan of attack, first, you will need to buy a software package. Then there is the time involved with training and getting up to speed. It may seem glamorous at the beginning, but then it can become a general pain when there are more pressing matters that need attention.

Next, you will need to find a Web hosting company, and that can cost anywhere from $10-30 per month. When looking for a hosting company, you should make sure that it is not someone who has servers in the basement. These servers should be with a large ISP (Internet Service Provider). The whole idea is to get someone who is reputable and who is going to be around for awhile. A word of caution: should your ISP go out of business and you don't get to them before and you don't have a back-up of your Web site, it is gone forever. This brings me to another point, you should keep a back-up copy of your Web site on your premises.

The third type is the non-traditional company. The only company that is out there like this is a company called OpenNet, Inc. (see Resource Guide for more information). This is the type of company that I went with. With OpenNet,

> You define the kind of Web site you want and the starting point that is the proposal you will receive (approximately $100/page). You will also get a schedule of costs to expand the site.

> There is no software to buy and training is provided as customers update their own site on a day-to-day basis. If technical support is needed there is usually no charge if the change take less than 5 minutes.

> Hosting is $30-50 per month with 100 e-mail addresses.

Elements of a Good Web Site

You need to answer the questions Who? What? Where? When? And How? Who you are? What services or products do your offer? Where are you located? When you are open - your hours of operation? How can a potential client contact you?

Your Web site should be easy to navigate. Some ways to avoid having that potential client get lost in your Web site and giving up altogether are your having a "Site Map" button which shows a map of the entire site and a "Find" function which allows searching for a particular word.

There is also a big discussion on the number of graphics it should have. According to Jim Green of OpenNet, Inc., the only companies that need to have a graphic-intensive Web site are graphics companies. Flash animation looks cool, but it can be costly to design and can take a long time to download. You don't want to put off an impatient potential client who is annoyed with waiting. Other companies should only have graphics for staff, products, and services.

Sites should be kept up to date. I can't tell you how many I saw while doing my research that had not been updated in 2 or 3 years. I didn't know what to think. Is the company still in business? Are the prices correct? Is the staff current? It kind of turned me off to that company because they were not professional enough to keep it up. So, if you are going to put "The Last Time This Site Was Updated" on your site make sure it is up-to-date.

Buy your own domain name!!! An article in one of the massage magazines featured Web sites that were sub-pages of someone else's Web site. This is a poor idea because it looks as if the business did not consider itself important enough to invest in its own site. I admit that I am not that Internet savvy, but I am sure that there are other people like me and those are lost clients because they gave up trying to find your site. It costs so little to register your name and maintain it on a yearly basis that I strongly recommend you do it.

How to Get Your Web Site Out There

Your Web site is just a part of your marketing plan, not in lieu of one. You Web address should be included on all printed material: brochures, business cards, reminder cards, letterhead, print advertising, and it should be included on your answering machine message. My message says, "You have reached MassageWorks. Our office hours are Monday through Friday from 10 – 6 p.m. If you have reached us during these hours, we are either with a client or on another line so please leave us a message and we will get back to you as soon as possible. For more information about MassageWorks, please visit our Web site at massageworksinc.com.

Register your domain name with as many complimentary sites as you can (i.e. associations you belong to). Also register with all major search engines (the top 20). You will find several of the ways to register quite costly for a quick turnaround and to have your listing higher up when the prospect does a search. I would register the free way because it is really not worth the money to get high on the list.

How to Register Your Name

First, you must figure out the name that you want. This task may be harder than you think because the name may already be taken. I had to go with "massageworksinc.com" because "massageworks.com" was already taken.

Second, you register with one of the companies listed below. Although there are about 1200 registrars worldwide, they all use the same master database.

VeriSign is about $35/year. This is the company I went through to get my domain name. I haven't had any problems with them, but several people have told me they had problems getting through to someone if they are experiencing a problem. I would imagine that this is because they are such a large company.

Register.com is about 32/year.

Buy Domains is $16/year. TheInternetDoctor.biz is a registered reseller for Buy Domains. They can also be reached at www.TheInternetDoctor.info or www.TheInternetDoctor.net.

To Have On-line Shopping or Not

It is my goal to make money while I sleep, which is one of the reasons I am writing this book, but it's also why I have an on-line shopping cart. I would hope that everyone seriously considers this because it allows you to be open 24 hours a day, 365 days a year without the expense of employees. You should be offering on-line the same products that you carry in your office.

You will need a merchant services account that allows on-line transactions. It usually costs around $1000 for set-up and then $60/month plus 2-3% per transaction.

If you have a merchant services account already, you can check to see if you can be set up for on-line transactions. If they don't, you have another option. You can get a security certificate allowing you to collect the customer information on-site in a secure environment and then process the transaction off-site as you currently do. This costs $150 to set-up; $125/year to renew and $10 per month for the IP address.

Horror Stories

A Web development company called a large regional shopping mall to say that it was going out of business for non-payment of bills. The mall was three days from launching a major on-line advertising campaign. This left them no e-mail and no on-line presence.

Solution: Ask for a list of existing clients and check three to five references and check amount of time in business.

A businesswoman paid $750 for a two-page Web site. The first page was to have a graphic image, and the second page was to have company information on it. She got a Web site with an ugly picture and incorrect information. When she asked for it to be corrected, she was told that it would cost $500. The site has never been changed.

Solution: Understand what you are buying. Be sure that you have a final say before completion (I would make sure that I had at least three chances to see the Web Site to make changes before signing off on the final). Also, don't pay for it all up front. I would pay only 50-60% with the signed contract and net upon completion.

An employee of a real estate company said that he could build the company's Web site for free. He had great ideas and set-up the site. That employee no longer works for the company, but the company has a site that is non-working and an embarrassment to the company.

Solution: Don't have a Web site done for free especially by an employee, friend, relative, or church member because it is not the person's top priority and often becomes a *non*-priority. You also can't fire pro bono and there is no contract.

My Experience With Web Site Advertising

Percentage of Clients:	24%
Percentage of Income:	12%
Percentage of Advertising:	17%
Cost Per Client:	$8.50

At the one-year mark we were 9.29%, 5%, 9.4%, and $27.97 respectively.

My Web site ranks second highest in total cost spent on advertising. This number includes the fee for the Web designer, the conversion fees to OpenNet, as well as the monthly hosting costs. While I did design my Web site, I don't know HTML and have no desire to learn. As it turned out, I met a person at a class I was taking who put what I gave her into HTML. She actually took her fee in trade. While there was no money that actually exchanged hands, I have included what it would have cost me because I did have to give her a fixed number of massages in trade that cost me money in opportunity costs.

The only cost associated with my Web site is my monthly hosting, which is $35 per month. This may seem high compared to the $9.95 and $14.95 per month rates you see advertised. You need to be careful with those because of the hidden costs. Also, my current provider allows me to make as many changes as I want without having to know HTML or paying him to do it.

Clients from the Web site have grown 87% from my one-year anniversary and represent 24% (2nd highest, first are clients resulting from my circle of influence) of all MassageWorks clients. Actually the Web site had not been in existence for a full year as it was not up and running until several months after I started business. I have averaged approximately 10 new clients per month from that site. This phenomenal growth has allowed the cost per client to decrease almost by $15, almost 64%.

Income has grown 85%. Income per month is approximately $1,000, while it costs only $35 to maintain. Return on investment is more that 28 times the cost.

If you haven't already guessed, I would definitely do this one again.

Other reasons to have an on-line presence:

Thirty-five percent of people purchasing gift certificates who were not clients came from finding me on the Internet;

I got a pretty healthy seated massage contract from a client that originated from a Web site gift certificate;

I have the opportunity to work with a local ballet company as a result of someone from California buying a gift certificate for a dancer in this company.

Other On-line Marketing Tools

In my research while I was developing my Web site, I ran across some of the following. You may want to look into them as well.

Yahoo Yellow Pages

Your local yellow pages may have their own version of on-line yellow pages

www.about.com

www.BodyZone.com

www.Massagereferral.com

www.Iwantamassage.com

www.Massageregister.com

Local information sites. In the Washington D.C. area, for example, there are dcpages.com, washingtonian.com, washingtonwoman.com and washingtonparent.com. One way to find these sites is to do a search on "massage" or "massage therapy" in your area and see what comes up.

Now that we have covered the methods I used and why I used them, let's look at how I decreased the amount of money I was spending on marketing efforts after the first year while increasing sales and maintaining or increasing the number of new clients each month.

Chapter 14

Spending Little or No Money Marketing

At the end of June 2001, I was giving a massage to a friend who had owned his own business for 20 years. After the massage, we were discussing expenses associated with owning a business. I asked him to take a look at my profit and loss statement to see if he could see any areas where I could improve. He said that I was doing very well, but posed the question "How well are your marketing dollars paying off?" Since I was in the process of writing the first version of this book after my one-year anniversary I had the statistics right at hand. My cost per client on average was $28.76. I didn't think that this was an excessive amount to pay for a client knowing that most companies expect to pay 10% of their expected gross revenue on marketing. The company I worked for in my previous career had spent $500 to get a customer.

His comment got me thinking. How could I reduce the amount of money I was spending while growing or maintaining my client base? As I thought about this opportunity, I had two thoughts roaming through my head. First, I know from previous reading that after about a year, you can slow down the amount of marketing you do for about three months to see if it has any effect on your business. Second, I have been studying metaphysics for the past few years and know that thoughts are very important. My thought was that I wanted to grow or maintain my current client base while spending little or no money on marketing.

As a result of his comments and "envisioning" my success without spending any money, I haven't spent any money on advertising since July 2001 with the following exceptions: my Yellow Pages display ad (which ran until December 2001); the commissions for SpaWish and Simply Certificates, and the monthly costs associated with my Web site. How? Simple. I wanted it. I made it a goal. I told the universe what I wanted. I became a magnet for that desire.

I am getting a head of myself. First, let me first fill you in on metaphysics and the universal laws surrounding it and then I will tell you the four "magic" steps to get what you want.

Definition of Metaphysics

Physics is "the study of matter and energy", while meta means to transcend or "see the situation behind something." Therefore metaphysics is the "study of matter and energy beyond the physical plane into other dimensions."

Purpose of Metaphysical Study

Metaphysical study helps you overcome limited thinking and become all you can be. The method of doing this is based on the study of ancient theories of how the universe was formed, how it operates, and man's purpose in it. Exercises in concentration, visualization and meditation are some of the means to help you focus and become comfortable in working with your mind.

Basic Metaphysical Principles

You are the director of your life. No outside force directs your actions and you are not a victim of anything! This basic metaphysical principle underlies all else that is written on metaphysics. What it states is that nothing external controls you. There is a part, an internal essence of you that is directing your thinking and your perception of the world.

So who is this controller and who put it in charge? The answer is the "Higher Self" within you, who has all knowledge and knows what your path in life is. The concept brings up some interesting questions and conflicts, for it is the principle of a "Higher Self" that often labels metaphysics as being a religion. Unfortunately, this concept is misinterpreted as saying that metaphysics negates a Divine Being or higher source of wisdom. The difference is the metaphysical perception of that source of wisdom.

Metaphysics teaches that there is one Deity, whatever your religious belief perceives that Being to be, and that Being is within you rather than apart from you. The part of you that is ever in contact with that Deity is the Higher Self. The Higher Self is constantly receiving energies from the Deity. These energies not only sustain your physical body, but also direct you to the life experiences you need for spiritual and personal growth.

Now that metaphysical understanding has been explained, here are the four steps to achieving your prosperous massage practice while spending little or no money on marketing.

I am assuming that you want greater success in marketing your business than you are receiving at the moment. If you were already enjoying all the success you desire, you would not have chosen to read this book. I also assume that you are prepared to do something about your present condition, as even reading this book takes some degree of effort.

This means that your desire for a better business is so strong that you are prepared to make whatever changes are necessary to enable it to happen.

Many of these changes are inside you. You might need to change your attitude towards yourself and others. If you harbor hatred, envy, or any other harmful emotion, you will have to release this negativity before you can attain your goals.

Maybe you think more negative thoughts than positive ones and need to change your way of thinking. Since we attract to ourselves what we think about, it is extremely important to stay in control of our thoughts.

You must have a strong desire. Most people are full of conflicting desires. They want this, they want that, but they don't want the other thing. They are like children deciding what they want for Christmas. It is fine to have several different goals, but they must be compatible with each other, and you must fervently desire them.

Much of the information presented below and in the next few chapters I learned from such experts as Richard Webster, a metaphysical teacher; Dr. Paul Yan, my Feng Shui Master, as well as other metaphysical teachers. I took their information and experimented with it culminating in the steps for attainment of goals. I hope you will be as interested and fascinated with the information as I was.

Here are the steps that lead you toward the attainment of your desires in your massage business:

Step 1. Dream what you want.

Step 2. Write the dream down.

Step 3. Tell the universe what you want

Step 4. Become a magnet that attracts your desires to you.

Chapter 15

Dream Big Dreams

Frequently, people think their dreams might be too ambitious and don't act on them. Don't think that way! You are underestimating yourself. If you have the ability to dream something, you also have the ability to make it happen. In fact, it is usually good to aim for a dream that is so ambitious it frightens you. This gives you an added edge that ultimately demolishes anything that stands in the path of your success.

You have a number of dreams every single night. Usually they are simply fantasies that never come true. To make the dream a reality, you need to follow all four steps in Chapter 14. When you write the dream down, you are in effect setting a goal for yourself. A dream normally fades away quickly and is forgotten, but when you articulate it in words, you are creating a record that will remind you of its existence every time you see the piece of paper.

In one sense, writing the dream down is telling the universe that you want this dream to become a reality. However, you need to do much more than that to ensure that your dream comes true.

Finally, you must be prepared to receive what you want. To do this you need to magnetize yourself so that your desires are attracted to you, while at the same time the things that you do not want are repelled.

This may seem too simple to be true. However, it works. I have done it. Since you can use this method to manifest any and all of your dreams, I feel compelled to tell you that there are a few precautions.

The most important is that your dreams hurt no one else. Naturally, most of your dreams will be for your own benefit, but you must ensure that no one will be hurt in the process. If, for example, your dream is to free yourself from a restrictive relationship, you should not wish any harm on the other person, no matter what that person may have done to you. Wish for the relationship to end, by all means, but phrase the request in such a way that no one is hurt. We will discuss how to phrase our requests shortly.

Wishing evil or harm on anyone else is black magic. You can use these techniques to hurt others, but the law of karma will then come into play, and you will ultimately suffer at least as much as the person you have harmed. We all reap what we sow. If you do a good deed, sooner or later something good will come back to you. Likewise, if you do a bad deed, sooner or later you will be made to pay for it. The law of karma is completely neutral and impartial.

How to determine what to ask for

Are you having trouble figuring out what are your dreams are? What does creating a prosperous practice mean to you? It may help to review your vision, business plan and marketing plan.

Chapter 16

Write it Down

From following the exercises in the previous chapter, you have a number of ideas about what you want. At the moment, they are simply dreams. What you need to do now is turn them into goals, complete with a plan of action of how you are going to achieve them.

It is a good idea to have a notebook to record all your ideas and dreams in. Write everything that occurs to you, no matter how unusual or impractical or farfetched it may seem. Something that seems impossible today may be easy to achieve six months from now. However, if you do not write it down, the thought is likely to disappear and never be realized.

Evaluate your ideas and categorize them into areas of your life: financial, mental, physical, social, spiritual, and intuitive. Number these ideas by degree of importance and then try to start with the most important one.

Your goal should be as specific as possible. Many people set goals that are far too vague. They say, for instance, they want to be rich. Although a worthy aim, it does not constitute a worthwhile goal by itself. It does make a good start toward setting a goal, and the true goal can be found by asking questions.

If, for instance, your goal is to become rich, there are several questions you can ask yourself. How rich do you want to be? Write a specific amount of money. What will you do to make this money? Is this something you enjoy doing? It will not be easy to make a great deal of money doing something you hate. How long will it take to make this amount? How will your life be different once you have this money? Will making this amount of money make you happy? What will I do once you have this money? Writing the answer to these, and any other questions that occur to you, will help you clarify your thoughts. This process will also reveal the price you will have to pay to achieve your goal. There is *always* a price.

It is important to write down the answers to all these questions. Once you have them recorded in your notebook you can then rewrite the main points as a goal. Someone who wants to become rich, for instance, might end up with the following goal: "I intend to succeed as a massage therapist and business owner and create a warm welcoming environment where people can come to relax or have their aches and pains worked on. I intend to make $100,000 a year from massage. To do this, I will do 29 massages per week for 50 weeks taking a 2-week vacation. I intend to make one million dollars in the next ten years. Once I have made one million dollars, I will buy my dream vacation home in Hawaii and devote at least a third of my time to helping people less fortunate than I am. Signed, John Smith."

This goal is clear and specific. John intends to make a million dollars in ten years. He knows how he is going to do it. He also knows what he is going to do with the money, once he has it. John has a plan but does not extend past 10 years into the future. At some stage, he will have to revise and modify his plan. Our lives are never static and something that is important to us now may be of no consequence later. Our plans should always be flexible, and we should not hesitate to change them when it feels right to do so.

The universe can sometimes put surprising situations in our paths, and we must be flexible enough to seize the good opportunities. Naturally, if you take that opportunity, you will need to set new goals.

The next stage is to send our desires out into the universe. We will start discussing this in the next chapter.

Chapter 17

Out into the Universe

We use the creative, universal energy that is present in everything and connects everything in the universe. Although we may think we are completely separate from each other and everything else in the universe, in realty we are all connected.

Throughout history, universal energy has been known by different names: Spirit, God, chi and prana are but a few. Universal energy is being created all the time. Every time you have a thought, you are creating universal energy. Idle thoughts create little energy, but focused thoughts have the power to change the world. Prayers, affirmations, and goals all create large amounts of universal energy. This universal energy cannot be destroyed yet it can be guided and transformed.

We know what we want. We must also have intention. We need to know what we want, but it is best if we allow the universe to manifest itself in the form that it decides. For instance, you may have a strong desire to marry. You may have the exact person you want firmly planted in your mind. However, if you become too fixed in this specific outcome, you may lose the possibility of a better result. Have a strong intent, but do not try to force a specific outcome.

When you send your desire or goal out into the universe you are using the natural laws of nature to attain your particular goal. Ideally, this goal will enrich you, the people around you, and your environment. By doing this, you are taking positive steps to control your own life. Your personal growth and development will speed up immensely as well. You will find your life rewarding, satisfying, and fulfilling. In the process, you will discover that you really can attain anything that you desire.

Ritual

A ritual is a procedure or a way of conducting a ceremony that enables you to achieve your dreams. Its purpose is to create the desired environment in which your dreams can manifest. A ritual should never be performed frivolously.

Rituals are common practice in organized religion. Prayer is considered a ritual. When we pray, we do so believing that whatever we pray for will be answered. When we perform a ritual, we also expect that the universal energy mentioned above, also called cosmic forces to provide us with whatever we ask for.

Ritual itself has enormous power, as it stimulates and energizes the cosmic forces and enables "magic" to occur. Ritual also stimulates and energizes the person conducting it by removing all doubt and negativity and providing enormous power and personal magnetism. This is why people appear transformed after participating in a ritual.

Some believe a ritual is something that is performed only in church, but we all perform small rituals all the time, probably every day. Don't believe me? Do you have a set way of getting ready in the morning? Do you always brush your teeth before you wash your face? Do you wait to drink your beverage until the end of the meal? If so, you practice rituals you have become accustomed to as the routine that works best for you.

Out into the Universe

You have written down exactly what you want. Now it is time to perform a ritual or ceremony to send it out into the universe, confident that your desires will be granted. There are many ways of doing this.

I will start with the first method I learned, and move on to some other alternatives I have used at different times. Why not stay with one method? Some requests seem to require a more formal approach to the universe than others. Sometimes, I prefer the "quick and easy" request, while on other occasions I prefer to make it more slowly. It is a matter of intuition.

There are a number of factors that need to be in place before you send your desire out into the universe: your environment, posture, and clothing. I will address those now.

The Best Places to Work

Naturally, the best place is anywhere you will not be disturbed and that is quiet, comfortable, and away from any distractions. If you live on your own, this may well be your living room. If other people live with you, it may be better to do this in your bedroom, or any room where you are unlikely to be disturbed. If the weather is mild, you may prefer to do this outside, again in a place where other people or extraneous noise will not disturb you.

Make the place suitable for what you are going to do. If you are indoors, tidy up the room and remove anything that could be a visual distraction. Make the room as sacred as possible. You may have a picture you can display, for instance. You may wish to place four white candles at the north, south, east, and west positions of the area you are working in. Alternatively, you might sprinkle a small amount of salt water in these directions.

If you are working outdoors, see if you can find a site close to a comfortable, protective tree. You can find "your" tree by hugging trees until you find one that responds to you. Do not hug every tree in sight, just those that appeal to you.

Once you have found your tree, clean up the area around it. This is a necessary preparation before sending your desire out into the universe, and it helps create a strong relationship between you and your protective tree.

Some people have a special rug to work on. This is fine, as it denotes a special area to work within. However, do not allow yourself to feel restricted to a particular area. If, for example, you are doing a walking meditation (to be explained shortly) you will need plenty of room to complete the ritual.

You might want to consider working on an altar. This can be a table that is used only for such purposes, or you may clear a table or shelf when necessary and use it when you are performing a ritual. To learn more about altars, I recommend Denise Linn's books *Altars* and *Creating Sacred Space*.

Posture

Naturally, you need to be comfortable. There are no rules about your body position, but it is usually better not to lie down. This is because you may fall asleep before sending your desires out into the universe. If I am outdoors, I usually kneel with my buttocks resting on the back of my legs. Indoors, I either kneel or sit in a straight-backed chair with the back of my hands resting on my thighs. I always begin this exercise with a meditation and find that I can do this easily and comfortably while in these positions.

Choose a position that is comfortable for you. As you need to be relaxed and free of stress and tension, it is important to be as comfortable as possible. Use pillows and anything else that ensures your comfort.

Clothing

Whatever you wear should be loose, comfortable, and preferably made of natural fibers. Restrictive clothing makes it hard to relax.

Although it may not always be possible, it is beneficial to have a bath or shower before starting. This is particularly important if you are asking for something that relates to long-term personal goals.

You are now ready to begin. Sending your desires out into the universe involves three steps:

> Relaxation and meditation (10-15 minutes)
> Mantra recitation (5-10 minutes)
> Sending out your desire (1-5 minutes)

Relaxation and Meditation

The first stage is to relax yourself as much as possible. Ensure that you will not be disturbed for at least 30 minutes, preferably longer. If you are doing this indoors, you should take the phone off the hook.

You may want to play gentle meditation-type music to help you relax as long as the music contains no recognizable melodies. If it does, you may find yourself humming along with the music rather than sending your desires out into the universe. If you play New Age music, it should not include the sound of running water, which can create a desire to visit the bathroom. Avoid any potential distractions of this sort.

Make sure the temperature is comfortable. You may wish to cover yourself with a blanket if you feel cool.

There is much misconception about meditation, including the notion that it is complicated. Meditation, however, is simply a matter of relaxing the body and mind to create a state of peace and serenity. This isn't easy at first and will require practice to be able to relax both the mind and the body and meditate for any length of time. We all become distracted with stray thoughts that unexpectedly come into our minds. Outside influences such as a sudden sound from another room can also take you mind off the meditation. While in a meditative state your metabolism, breathing, and heartbeat all slow down. Your brain waves move from the beta state, which is your normal state of consciousness, to the more peaceful alpha state, revealing an altered state of consciousness.

Of course, although it is pleasant and beneficial to relax your mind and body in this way, it is not true meditation yet. The ultimate aim is to achieve total mindfulness (where you are totally present). At this stage, enlightenment can occur, and it is a misconception to think meditation is simply another method of self-development. True meditation places you in direct contact with the universal forces and enables you to grow in knowledge and wisdom. It provides serenity of mind and opportunities for spiritual growth. It also creates the perfect opportunity for you to request from the universe whatever it is you want.

There are countless ways to meditate. I usually like to sit upright in a comfortable chair with a firm, straight back. My feet are flat on the floor and my spine is erect. You may think you would feel more comfortable in a soft armchair, but your spine will be curved and you will not be able to meditate for long without some discomfort.

I like to rest my hands in my lap, palms facing upward, with the right hand resting on the left palm and the tips of both thumbs touching each other. Some prefer to meditate with their hands resting on their thighs.

You might choose to meditate lying on your back, but if you do, I recommend it be on the floor rather than in bed. If you are lying in bed, you might be inclined to fall asleep.

Make yourself comfortable and close your eyes. Take three deep breaths. Count silently and slowly from one to four as you inhale, count to four again as you hold your breath, and then exhale slowly to the count of eight.

Once you have taken three breaths, forget about the counting but continue breathing slowly and deeply. Imagine a wave of relaxation slowly spreading over your entire body, from the top of your head down to the tips of your toes. Feel the relaxation enter every part of your body as it slowly drifts downward.

There is no need to hurry this process. Simply allow every part of your body to relax. Once you have done this, mentally check your body for any remaining areas of tension, and allow them to relax. Most people find the tension in their necks and shoulders to be the hardest to release. If you feel that this may be you, before you begin to meditate, purposely shrug your shoulders and hold them as tightly against the sides of your neck as you can. After a few seconds, release them. Repeat 3-4 times. You will notice your shoulders have become much more relaxed.

Once you feel that your body is completely relaxed, focus your attention on your nostrils. Feel your breath coming in and going out. Concentrate on your breathing. Naturally, odd thoughts will pop into your mind from time to time. This is perfectly normal, and there is no need to worry when this occurs. All you need to do is acknowledge them and let them go and then return your focus to your breathing. Ultimately, there will be no thoughts. Once this point is reached, you are ready to recite your mantra.

As I mentioned earlier, it takes time and practice to become proficient at meditation. However, being able to meditate is of supreme importance. It allows you to reach your Higher Self, which is the God within you. Whatever it is that you desire can then be implanted in the deepest part of your subconscious mind, and whatever is placed there will ultimately manifest itself in your life.

Take whatever time is necessary to master this skill. Do not become concerned if your mind keeps wandering while you are meditating. Everyone experiences this. It can be extremely difficult to quiet our minds and temporarily forget about the worries and pressures of daily life, but regular daily practice, at the same time every day if possible, will ensure ultimate success.

Other Methods of Meditation

Color Meditation

There are many ways to achieve the right meditative state for sending your desires out into the universe. Many of you may recognize what I am about to describe as the "chakra" meditation as the colors reflect each of the chakras in order from first chakra to the seventh chakra.

Sit in a comfortable position with your eyes closed. Take three deep breaths and say to yourself, "Relax, relax deeply" each time you exhale. Remain aware of your breathing and feel the relaxation in your body.

Next, imagine yourself surrounded by a cloud of energy that is the most beautiful red your have ever seen. Allow yourself to become completely immersed in this red, and let it permeate every cell of your body.

Gradually allow the red to slowly fade and be replaced by orange, again the most vibrant shade of orange you have ever seen. Allow this orange to reach every part of your body, so that you are completely enfolded by it, both inside and out. Once you reach this state, allow the orange to fade and replace it with yellow. Allow this reach every fiber of your being and, in turn, replace it with green, followed by blue, indigo, and finally violet.

Once your have experienced the sensations of each color of the rainbow, allow the violet to disappear, and imagine yourself bathed in pure while light.

Golden Light Meditation

Make yourself comfortable, close your eyes, and take three deep breaths. Feel the pleasant relaxation in your body.

Now visualize a beautiful ball of golden light a few inches above your head. Watch this light slowly coming down and entering the top of your head. Feel the golden light relaxing every part of your body that it reaches. Feel it slowly moving down your body, relaxing every cell it meets on the way.

Finally, allow the ball of gold light to bathe your feet in its wonderful, soothing, restful glow. Allow it to remain there for about a minute, and then allow it to rise up through your body again, until it is back in position just above your head.

If needed, you can do this exercise two or three more times, becoming more and more relaxed each time.

Counting Backward Meditation

Relax comfortably with your eyes closed. Picture a large blank movie screen in your mind. Imagine that the number 100 is written on this screen in huge numbers. Look at this number and then allow it to dissolve until is has completely disappeared from your mind. Now, imagine the number 99 written on the screen. Again make this number dissolve and disappear. Continue to count down from one hundred until you feel that you are relaxed enough in both body and mind to start reciting the mantra. Usually, I am completely relaxed by the time I reach ninety, though there have been times when I have reached sixty before I can move to the next stage.

Walking Meditation

It is perfectly possible to mediate while walking. In fact, you have probably done it many times without knowing it. If you have ever walked anywhere while you were preoccupied, you have performed a walking meditation.

I find it easiest to do a walking meditation while silently repeating a mantra to myself (see the following section of examples). The mantra should be repeated in time with your footsteps, and is a highly effective and rapid way of achieving a totally relaxed state. Yes, you can be relaxed while you are moving.

Mantra Recitation

Mantra recitation is arguably the best-known form of meditation. A mantra is a short phrase or sentence that is repeated, usually aloud, over and over again.

According to one of my yoga teachers, the most famous mantra is "*Om mani padme hum*", which is usually translated as "O, thou jewel of the lotus." *Mani* can represent anything precious, including an enlightened mind. *Padme* represents the lotus blossom, as well as spiritual awakening. As *Om* represents the universal body, in this mantra we have body, mind and spirit.

Om is pronounced "aum". This word has special significance, for when it is spoken it begins from the deepest part of the throat and ends with the lips closed. The word *Om* depicts the universal cosmic consciousness. *Mani padme* is pronounced "mah-nee pahd-may," and *hum* is pronounced "haum", as it is a variation of *Om.*

To say the mantra, take a long deep breath. Half the exhalation is used to say "Om," followed by "mani padme," and a lengthy "hum" at the end.

You will feel a powerful vibration, almost like a hum, as you say this mantra. As you repeat it over and over again you will gradually feel more and more in tune with the infinite. This is the purpose of using mantras. They open up doorways to unseen worlds, and provide access to the universal life force. Mantras also help you to gain peace of mind and contentment.

Om mani padme hum is not only the best overall mantra to use, it can be used on all occasions. However, you can create your own mantra using any phrase that appeals to you. Some mantras consist of groups of syllables that have no particular meaning. It is the rhythm and pitch of the chant that make them work. Other mantras I have used are the following ones I learned from Thomas Ashley-Farrand in his work, *The Power of Mantras.*

One is a short version and the other is a longer version, and both versions work. They were derived from Lakshmi, the feminine principle of abundance. Ashley-Farrand states, "Repetition of the Shrim mantra produces the ability to attract and maintain abundance: financial wealth, good health, friends, enough food to eat, inner peace, the love of children and family, and so forth."

The short version is to say "Shrim" (pronounced "shreem") over and over again. The longer version is to say "Om Shrim Maha Lakshmiyei

Namaha". Ashley-Farrand states that if you are older than 28, replace "Namaha" with "Swaha" at the end of the mantra.

You should repeat your mantra for five to ten minutes. Mantras are extremely useful as a form of meditative device, and at the end of the time you will be in the perfect state to make your request.

Sending Out Your Request

The method I was taught is simple and effective. Write your wish on a piece of paper and set fire to it. As it burns, imagine your desire going out into the universe.

Once your request has completely burned, thank the universe for all your blessings. I prefer to spend a few minutes enjoying the pleasant feelings of relaxation before returning to full consciousness. I allow myself to think about my request, before becoming aware of my surroundings. When I open my eyes, I usually stretch as if waking from a restful sleep.

Many people like to end their rituals formally. How you do this is entirely up to you. You may like to make formal bow to each of the four cardinal directions. If you have burned candles in each of these areas, blow them out immediately after bowing in each of their directions.

There is no need to spend any more time thinking about your request. It has gone out into the universe and all you need is to remain confident that it will be granted. Some people find it almost anticlimactic to end on this note. If you are one of these people, you can hug yourself and shout, "It's mine! It's mine! It's mine!"

Some Alternative Methods

If the preceding method does not resonate with you, you can try one of these other methods.

Candle Burning

Another method of sending your request by burning a candle that has your request inscribed on the sides. Naturally, your request has to be written in as few words as possible.

You should use candles in white, red or gold for this purpose, as they relate to good luck and money in China.

Dressing the Candle

When you are ready to send your message out into the universe, wipe the candle carefully with good-quality olive oil. Use a fine cloth, and always wipe the oil onto the candle from the center out to the two ends. Start at the middle of the candle and work your way up to the top. Then, again starting from the middle, rub the candle down to the bottom.

This process is called "dressing" the candle, and you should think about your purpose in using the candle as you do it. This can become almost a ritual in itself, and is an essential part of the process. If you use the same candle a number of times, you must dress the candle with oil each time.

The purpose of this is to remove any negativity from the candle that may have been caused while it was being made or absorbed between the time of its manufacture and your buying it.

Blessing the Candle

Once the candle has been cleansed, it should be blessed. Place it on your right palm and rest this palm on your left palm. This creates a circle of energy. Close your eyes and think of your purpose in burning the candle. Visualize yourself as you will be once the request has come to fruition. Bless the candle for its part in the process. Finally, thank the architect of the universe for enabling your dreams to become manifest. Take a deep breath and say "Thank you" three times as you exhale. It makes no difference if you say these words silently or aloud.

Burning the Candle

It is best to burn the candle when it is dark outside. Place it on your home altar if you have one. Otherwise clear a table and place it in the center. If you like, you may cover your altar with a special cloth.

Light the candle and then turn off the lights in the room. Sit in a position that allows you to look directly at the flame. As the smoke drifts upward, think about your request and how the smoke is taking it out into the universe.

Watching the smoke for as long as you feel comfortable. I find about 30 minutes is right for me. Extinguish the flame either by covering the wick or using your figures to pinch the flame. Don't blow it out.

Your request is not completely transmitted until the entire candle has been consumed, so you will need to perform this ritual several times until the candle has completely burned down. However, word of your request will have gone out into the universe from the moment you light the candle the first time. Consequently, you should regard each additional session as reinforcement of the original one. I prefer to burn a candle over a period of successive days and find the repetition comforting and reassuring. If I am overly tired or feeling stressed one evening, I will postpone the burning until a time when I feel relaxed and in control. If possible, burn your candle over a series of evenings, but it's all right if you don't perform the ritual on consecutive nights.

Feng Shui

It is beyond the scope of this book to go fully into Feng Shui, so I will give a brief synopsis of what it is and how is relates to wealth and getting what you want.

Feng Shui (pronounced FUNG SHWAY), the Chinese art of placement, means "wind and water" and has been practiced in China for over 3000 years.

The earliest Feng Shui practitioners were priests who located auspicious sites to build villages. They relied on their intuition, their senses and the knowledge that had been passed down to them from their teachers. Feng Shui practitioners assessed the land using the following building blocks.

Chi

Chi (pronounced chee) is the first building block. Everything in the physical world is endowed with the living energy called Chi. This includes inanimate objects such as vehicles, gadgets, jewelry, and furniture as well as living things such as people, animals, and plants. Terah Kathryn Collins in her book *Western Guide to Feng Shui* succinctly expressed what I feel about what we "own" when she said, "Obviously, when we look around and see everything surrounding us as being "alive" it becomes vastly more important to live with things we feel good about."

Chi governs the universe and connects every physical thing. We all live in an interconnected web in which each thing is connected to another. An illustration of this is the following: If you throw a rock into a pond, the

84

whole surface of the water will be affected with ever-widening concentric ripples, and the water beneath the ripples will be altered as well.

There is constant change in all living things. We see this happening in everything from our bodies to the seasons. Even though things are constantly changing they strive to maintain a balance between the two extremes of yin and yang. Yin and yang are opposite yet complementary forces. While yin can be defined as feminine, back, dark, cool, earth, moon, yang is masculine, front, light, hot, sky, and sun. Ideally the two are in 50/50 balance to maintain peace and harmony.

The Five Elements Applied to Feng Shui

Just as we are comprised of yin and yang, we are also comprised of five elements. They are Fire, Earth, Metal, Water and Wood. As with yin and yang, it is best when the five elements are in balance; 20% of each would be ideal.

Each of these elements has a rich spectrum of associations, including shape, color, direction, taste, emotion and area of the body. They are expressed in the Figure 1 on the next page.

Fire	Earth	Metal	Water	Wood
Triangular	Square and Flat	Round or Arched	Wavy or Irregular	Narrow and Columnar
Red, purple, orange,	Yellow or Brown	White, gold, Silver/	Blue or Black	Green
South	Center, Southwest, Northeast,	West and Northwest	North	East and Southeast
Bitter, tart	Sweet, rich	Pungent, Spicy, hot	Salty	Sour, Vinegar
Joy, Excitement	Over-thinking	Grief	Fear	Anger
Heart and Small intestines	Stomach, Spleen	Lungs, large Intestines, colon	Kidneys, Bladder Reprod. Organs,	Liver and Gallbladder

Figure 1

The easiest way to work with the five elements in your environment is to observe which ones are missing and try to bring them into balance.

The Nourishing and Controlling Cycles

In the Nourishing Cycle, there is a Grantor, the nourishing element, and the element being nourished, called Offspring. You could look at is as a mother (grantor) and child (offspring) relationship in which the mother gives life to the child.

Grantor	Offspring
Fire creates	Earth
Earth protects	Metal
Metal produces	Water
Water nourishes	Wood
Wood generates	Fire

The opposite of this is the Controlling Cycle, one in which there is control and domination. In this cycle, there is a ruling element called Ruler and the element being ruled called Subordinate.

Ruler	Subordinate
Fire melts	Metal
Metal cuts	Wood
Wood checks	Earth
Earth absorbs	Water
Water puts out	Fire

Sometimes the Controlling Cycle is one of the most appealing ways to achieve elemental harmony and should really not be considered negative. For instance if your Fire element is too strong, you could introduce a Metal object which will decrease Fire's strength because it is busy trying to melt the Metal.

Bagua Map

The Bagua Map originated from the I Ching, which is an ancient Chinese book of divination. The word Bagua describes the eight trigrams of the I Ching. Each trigram is associated with the areas of your life such as: wealth, fame, love, family, health, children, self-knowledge, career and travel. Figure 2 depicts the Bagua Map.

Wealth and Prosperity	Fame	Love and Relationships
Green/Purple/Red Hip/Pelvis/Bones	Red Eyes South Fire	Red/Pink/White Organs/Mother
Family and Past	Health	Children and Creativity
Green Feet East Wood	Yellow/Brown Everything else Center Earth	White Mouth West Metal
Self Knowledge and Spirituality	Career	Helpful People and Travel
Black/Blue/Green Hands	Black/Blue Ears North Water	White/Gray/Black Head/Father

Figure 2

You can overlay the Bagua Map on any lot, building, house, apartment, room, or piece of furniture.

Place it so that the bottom three squares are next to your stomach. Next stand at the door and look into the room, building or piece of furniture. If there is more than one door into the room, stand at the one most frequently used. Remember, you will always enter any lot, building, house, or room from one of these three guas: Self-Knowledge and Spirituality, Career or Helpful People and Travel.

There are two forces that come in to play by overlaying the Bagua. The first is the timeless wisdom that the I Ching provides. The second is the user's serious intention to produce a positive change in his or her life. When a person places objects that are personally meaningful in areas correlated with the Bagua Map with intention (you must know what you want it to do for you) the chi is aligned to produce the results. I have seen some changes take place instantly and others taking longer to materialize.

Once when I activated the wealth section of my house, changes took places within minutes of my finishing. This was before I had an office and was then doing massage out of my home. I had a pretty steady clientele but noticed that the phone had stopped ringing and my appointments had dried up for a couple of days. I put on my Feng Shui eyes and started looking around to see what could be the matter. My dining room is in the wealth section of my house and, sorry to say, it had become a little cluttered. Clutter is not good! This topic is beyond the scope of this book. (If you are interested in learning more about clutter and how it affects you, please read Karen Kingston's book *Clear your Clutter with Feng Shui*.) Back to my story. I know that Chi comes into the house, makes it way to the center and then disperses out to each area. By having a cluttered dining room, I had limited my good in that area. In this case, my wealth. So I set about clearing my clutter and put a pretty jade plant on the table that had been moved. Within minutes after I finished cleaning and clearing, the phone rang and a client made an appointment.

Enhancements for Wealth and Prosperity

The following are enhancements and affirmations that will activate your Wealth section and affect wealth and prosperity in your life. Place these items in the wealth sections of your room, house (or apartment), or piece of furniture with intention. Here are some personal enhancements to chose from:

Items that "call in the Chi" such as wind chimes, windsocks or anything that moves and appeals to you.

Valuable possessions and collections that represent wealth and abundance to you. These could be any of the following: jewelry, antiques, art, sculpture, coins, crystal or silver.

Posters, paintings, collages, photos and figures that depict desired possessions such as homes, cars, boats, equipment, jewelry.

Blue, purple and red items.

Healthy plants, especially with shiny, rounded, coin-shaped leaves, such as jade (also known as the "Money tree"), or plants that bloom in the Wealth colors of reds, purples, and blues (i.e. African violet)

Fresh and silk flowers in reds, purples, and blues. You should avoid dried flowers as they have the chi robbed from them.

Water features, such as fountains and waterfalls, symbolizing the abundant flow of money and prosperity.

Quotations, affirmations, and sayings pertaining to wealth and prosperity. A few examples are:

"I am rich and prosperous in every way."

"Wealth and prosperity manifest easily and joyfully into my life, now and always."

"I attract abundance easily and effortlessly."

Just as there are items you would want in that particular area to enhance, there are also some things you will want to avoid in this area. They are:

Clutter

Dirt and dust

Broken items

Reminders of being without money or other bad times

Trash cans

Dead plants. If a plant does happen to die, remove it immediately and replace it with a healthy plant of the same size or bigger. The reason you must do this is the chi from the dead plant will remain until you do something to get rid of it.

Bathrooms (keep toilet lids closed when they are not in use. Close drains in sinks and tubs. Place a red ribbon around the outgoing pipes of your plumbing).

Now we have the building blocks of Feng Shui, let's explore how we can use it to get want we want.

Getting what we Want Using Feng Shui

Just to reiterate for a moment, most people don't get what they want because they haven't defined exactly what it is they want. What do you want out of life? Just take one minute (you can take more if you like; you can even do this same exercise for each of the areas on the Bagua) and explore what you want for your business (wealth). First, get into a comfortable position. Next, take a few deep breaths. Finally, if you knew that you could not fail and money was no object, what would you want for your business? Dream big!

Write down what you want here:

_____

_____

_____

_____

_____

Next use the building blocks of Feng Shui to help materialize that desire. Whatever items you decide to use to activate your Wealth section, you should use with intention. For instance, I decided to place a jade plant on my dining room table (remember my Dining Room happens to be in my Wealth Section). Before I placed the plant, I had my desired goal firmly planted in my mind and visualized this jade plant as being the representation of my goal. Now every time I see the jade plant it has two purposes: On a conscious level, it is a reminder to me of my desired goal. On a subconscious level, I have visualized my goal already happening. Remember the subconscious mind doesn't know the difference between what is real and what is not, so it will do everything it can to make your desire a reality.

Chapter 18

Magnetizing Yourself

It may seem strange that you write down your request, create a ritual to send it out into the universe, and then simply stop. In a sense, you are really not stopping. You need to maintain a sense of positive expectancy that your request will be granted. You should have no doubt whatsoever that what you asked for will happen. After all, at the very deepest level, your will is also your Creator's will. Therefore, the architect of the universe will grant your request.

There is an interesting concept known as "luck". Some people seem to have good luck all the time, while others are cursed with bad luck. No matter how unlucky you may have been in the past, the techniques I have just described will enable you to become one of the lucky ones. I believe that we create our own destiny by the way we think. If you consider yourself unlucky, that is what you will receive until you change your thoughts. Lucky people have a positive expectancy. They expect good things to happen to them, and they invariably do.

It is natural to feel despondent when things don't work the way we want them to. However, even in these situations naturally lucky people think, "It didn't work this time, but next time it will." These people quickly get over their depression and start planning again. They expect good things to happen to them, and of course, that is exactly what they receive.

There is no knowing how long it will take for your desires to become realized. Usually, simple requests are manifested quickly, while more complex desires take longer. However, this is not always the case. It is vital that you remain positive while you are waiting for your requests to be granted. Naturally, you will experience doubt and uncertainty at times. Whenever you catch yourself thinking negatively, remind yourself that the matter is now in the hands of the universe and it will happen. These negative feelings will occur far less frequently once you magnetize yourself.

A magnet both attracts and repels. Naturally, you want to repel any negative energy that prevents you from achieving your goals. Likewise, you want positive energy that propels you toward your goals.

It is important to magnetize yourself so strongly that any thoughts of failure vanish before they are fully formed. Your mind must remain calm, serene, and supremely confident that your desire will be granted. There are many ways of doing this.

Thoughts, Feelings, and Emotions

While you are waiting for your request to become a reality, spending time thinking about how your life will be different once it is achieved. In your mind's eye see as clearly as possible the beneficial changes that will take place. Picture yourself enjoying the pleasures and advantages of your new life. Think about your request when you have a few spare moments.

Become aware of your feelings and emotions concerning your request. Naturally, you will have considerable emotional attachment to a positive outcome. Allow these feelings and emotions to fully play when thinking about your goals. Desires that have an emotional component are always more successful than requests that have been worked out only clinically or logically.

Be careful that your thoughts, feelings and emotions do not become negative during this time. What goes on in our heads, really affect us in a tremendous way. Here is an exercise to illustrate this point:

Working with a friend, hold your dominant arm out to the side at shoulder level and have the friend push down on your hand. The point at which is your baseline measurement. Now say, "I am a weak and worthless person" ten times. Have your friend recheck your strength. You will find that you won't be able to resist as you could before. It is amazing that just by saying these few words (you didn't even have to say them with emotion), your subconscious mind believed you and made it so. You don't want to stay in this condition, so say, "I am a strong and vibrant person" ten times. Recheck. You should be back to your original strength.

Let me add a side note. I have begun to monitor the television shows I watch, music I listen to as well and what I read. I don't want anything negative to affect my subconscious. I would recommend that you do the same, especially during this period of goal achievement.

Affirmations

Another method is to use affirmations as frequently as possible. Affirmations are positive suggestions that are deliberately implanted into the subconscious mind. Affirmations also remind us that we need to keep aware of our thoughts and that we alone are responsible for our actions. We all have some fifty to sixty thousand thoughts a day and many of these are negative. As we become what we think about, it is important to think more positive thoughts than negative ones. Whenever you find yourself thinking something negative, switch it around and make it positive, or say an affirmation to yourself. It can be helpful to remember that our thoughts create our reality. We need to make sure we are thinking as many positive thoughts as possible.

You can say affirmations to yourself at any time. They are more effective when said aloud, as this enables you to hear them as you say them. You can repeat them in different ways, for example, by placing the emphasis on different words each time. However, affirmations can also be used silently.

Affirmations should be phrased in the present tense, as if you already have the quality or thing you desire. Here are some general affirmations that you can use. It is a good idea to write out your own affirmations that relate specifically to you and your desires. You should carry these around with you so you can read them in spare moments. Here are some examples,

> "I attract nothing but good into my life."
> "I am successful."
> "I am a loving and caring person."

These are general, all-purpose affirmations that can be extremely helpful. However, you should also compose specific affirmations that relate to you and your specific desires.

I used a particular affirmation to achieve my desired goal of maintaining a certain level of clients while spending little or no money on marketing. It was the following: "I am so happy and grateful now that clients come to me in increasing numbers through multiple sources using little or no money to obtain these clients on a continuous basis."

I also say the following every morning when I first wake up. "I am fully booked attracting to me the clients who need and want my services." Sometimes I will have only two clients booked when I get to work, but by the end of the day, I will have been fully booked. For me, fully booked is five appointments per day.

Your subconscious mind cannot tell the difference between this imaginary picture and reality, and will work to make it become part of your life. Try it and see what happens!

Visualization

Shakti Gawain has a fine book called *Creative Visualization*, which I recommend you read. Simply put, visualization is like playing a movie in your mind of your goal as if it is already reality. So take time to visualize your goal with emotion as if it has already happened. Joseph Murphy states in *The Power of Your Subconscious Mind,* "The subconscious cannot reason like your conscious mind. Your subconscious mind cannot argue controversially. Hence, if you give it wrong suggestions, it will accept them as true and will proceed to bring them to pass as conditions, experiences, and events." And the opposite is also true. If you put in worthy suggestions that you want and believe to be true, your subconscious will do all it can to make them true as well.

If you are having difficulty visualizing something, you can write it down as if you are giving a synopsis of your business to be included in a newspaper.

I learned the following technique from my coach, Nina East. I wanted to be able to visualize a full schedule, but was having difficulty. Nina suggested that I write in my appointment book the word "client" wherever I wanted to have an appointment. I wanted appointments at 10 a.m., 11:30 a.m., 2:00 p.m., 3:30 p.m., and 5:00 p.m., so next to each of those times, I wrote "client" if I didn't already have someone in that time slot. What this does it allow your mind to see a full appointment book and allowing it to manifest itself. Joseph Murphy, in *The Power of Your Subconscious Mind*, wrote "Remember always, that what you are seeking is also seeking you." You will just have to be careful when someone is trying to schedule that you are cognizant of what is really available. Try it and see how it works for you.

Talismans

A talisman is an object that is believed to possess magical properties. They are frequently made from parchment, papyrus, pottery, or shell, but can also be made from stone or metal. They are intended to bring about a specific result from an event that has not yet occurred. Talismans can actually be made of anything: something as simple as a pebble found on the beach or a sheet of paper containing words of protection. Of course, they can also be ornate and valuable like a necklace or ring. Traditionally, they were made of precious stones or valuable metal and were worn to provide protection and to ward off the "evil eye."

Talismans could be described as good luck charms. People have carried such charms on them for thousands of years, both to create good luck and to avert bad luck.

It is not necessary to go to great lengths to find a ring or other piece of jewelry, you can simply use the stone that relates to your zodiac sign or birth month.

Here are the most common stones for the birth month.

> January – garnet
> February – amethyst
> March – aquamarine, bloodstone
> April -- diamond, sapphire
> May – emerald
> June – pearl, moonstone, cat's eye, turquoise, agate
> July – ruby, turquoise, onyx
> August – peridot, carnelian, moonstone, topaz
> September – sapphire, chrysolite
> October – opal, beryl, tourmaline
> November – topaz
> December – turquoise, ruby, bloodstone, lapis lazuli

You may prefer to use the stone that relates to your astrological sign:

> Aries – diamond, ruby, red jasper
> Taurus – lapis lazuli, sapphire
> Gemini – citrine, yellow agate
> Cancer – pearl, moonstone
> Leo – tiger's-eye
> Virgo – green jasper
> Libra – sapphire, aquamarine
> Scorpio – ruby, opal, red jasper
> Sagittarius - topaz
> Capricorn – turquoise, smoky quartz
> Aquarius - amethyst
> Pisces – moonstone, rose quartz

Or you may prefer to find a stone that resonates with you. I personally have a diamond heart pendant as my talisman because is reminds me that "I am love" and that "Love is always with me."

The purpose of talismans is that every time you see yours, it becomes more and more embedded in your consciousness, and since we all attract to us what we think about, we are likely to achieve our goals.

Reiki

Assuming you have at least Reiki First Degree, you can use it to magnetize your good to you. You have your affirmation or desired goal (if you don't, you should do it now) written on a piece of paper. Carry that piece of paper with you, and when you can bring it out, hold it in your hands and Reiki the paper and all that is signifies.

If you have Reiki Second Degree, you can repeat the steps above, but to give it added strength you can use one of the symbols over the piece of paper. I like using the "power sandwich."

Show Your Gratitude

While you are waiting for your request to be answered, think of how you will express your gratitude to the universe. Thank the universe in advance for granting your request. Decide exactly what you are going to do to express your gratitude. The more you give of yourself, the more you will receive in return. Give abundantly and you will receive abundantly. This giving may bear no direct relationship with your request, but it is still a form of expressing your gratitude to the universe for giving you what you want.

Afterword

I hope you are now aware of some very powerful methods to bring what you want into your life and into your business. My business was totally transformed at the same time I saved thousands of dollars over the past two years. What were my results? I haven't advertised since July 2001, yet I have increased my business an average of forty clients per month since I stopped advertising.

Would I change anything I have done in the past three years? I don't think I would. Even though I knew about these methods of getting what you want before I started my business, I still decided to go the traditional route. The clients that came to me through traditional marketing methods have been a blessing, and we have formed warm relationships and strong friendships. My regret, though, is that I didn't stick with some of what I have told you here. I let others sway me from my path, and many of those ventures turned out to be failures. So remember to make a plan and work your plan.

Now you must take what you have learned here, continue to study and learn as much as you can about metaphysical thought. And then watch what happens.

But nothing will happen unless you decide what you want, write it down, send it out to the universe, and magnetize yourself.

In Catherine Ponder's book, *Prosperity Secrets of the Ages,* she wrote, "You, too, can have everything!" I wish you great success as you go for your dreams.

Appendix A

Thanks for the Referral

Thanks for referring John Doe. In appreciation, please use this certificate for 10% off your next massage, facial or body treatment ($10 maximum discount) at MassageWorks. Call today to schedule your next appointment. This offer cannot be combined with any other offer and expires January 31, 2003. Please bring this certificate to receive your discount.

MassageWorks
450 W. Broad Street, Suite 412
Falls Church, VA 22046
(703) 536-7200

Sample Gift Certificate

No.:
Date: _____

MassageWorks Gift Certificate

To: _____

This entitles you to

compliments of _____

Message:

SAMPLE

_____   _____
Expiration Date   Authorized Signature

MassageWorks -- (703) 536-7200

Sample Follow-up Letter

MassageWorks, Inc.
450 W. Broad Street
Falls Church, VA 22046
(703) 536-7200

Dear Client:

Thank you for your recent visit to MassageWorks. In an effort to serve you better, we have created a client survey form to get your overall impressions of MassageWorks and how we can better serve you.

Please take a moment to fill out the enclosed client survey form and return it in the enclosed self-addressed stamped envelope.

We appreciate your time in filling out our survey and have enclosed a coupon for $5 off your next service at MassageWorks.

Sincerely,

Linda Steele
President

Sample Client Survey Form

| | MassageWorks Client Survey | Please return to: MassageWorks 450 West Broad Street #412 Falls Church VA 22046 |

Please indicate the service(s) that you received at MassageWorks.

☐ Body Treatment   How often have you had this type of service in the past? ☐ 1-10 ☐ 11+

☐ Facial   How often have you had this type of service in the past? ☐ 1-10 ☐ 11+

☐ Manicure   How often have you had this type of service in the past? ☐ 1-10 ☐ 11+

☐ Massage   How often have you had this type of service in the past? ☐ 1-10 ☐ 11+

☐ Pedicure   How often have you had this type of service in the past? ☐ 1-10 ☐ 11+

Please rate your experience.

Overall impression of MassageWorks   ☐ Excellent ☐ Good ☐ Average ☐ Poor

Suggested improvements: _____

Overall impression of your therapist, esthetician, or nail technician

☐ Excellent ☐ Good ☐ Average ☐ Poor

To insure quality service of all our practitioners, include his/her name: _____

Suggested improvements: _____

How did your experience at MassageWorks compare with previous experiences for the same type of service?   ☐ Excellent ☐ Good ☐ Average ☐ Poor

Suggested improvements: _____

Would you recommend MassageWorks to a friend? ☐ Yes   ☐ No

Were all members of MassageWorks staff polite and professional? ☐ Yes ☐ No

How did you hear about MassageWorks?

☐ Print Media   ☐ Friend   ☐ massageworksinc.com

☐ Gift Certificate   ☐ Yellow Pages   ☐ Bioelements.com

☐ Other _____

Website

Have you visited our website? (www.massageworksinc.com)   ☐ Yes   ☐ No

How often do you visit to learn about the monthly specials and/or classes?

☐ Once a month   ☐ Occasionally   ☐ Never

Additional comments:

Sample $5 Off Coupon

Thank you for taking the time to
Respond to our client survey
Bring this coupon in to take $5 off your next service
At MassageWorks

Not valid with any other offers. Expires _____.

MassageWorks, Inc.
450 W. Broad Street, #412
Falls Church, VA 22046
(703) 536-7200
www.massageworksinc.com

Happy Birthday

This entitles you to $10 off your next massage, facial or body treatment from MassageWorks

Call today to schedule your next appointment. This offer cannot be combined with any other offer and expires August 31, 2003.

Please bring this certificate to receive your discount.

MassageWorks
450 W. Broad Street, Suite 412
Falls Church, VA 22046
(703) 536-7200

MassageWorks E-Newsletter
March 2003

Welcome everyone to this month's E-Newsletter.

In this edition you will find:
Special of the Month
What's New
Therapeutic Aromatherapy Study Group
Tips and Tidbits
Coaches Corner
Schedule of Classes
a carol on Stretching Yourself by Carol Goldsmith
Contact Us and Disclaimer

Please feel free to pass this newsletter on to whomever you think might benefit from it. Enjoy!

Special of the Month

Siddha Body Detoxificiation　　　　　　**Regularly $75; now $70**

The Siddha Body Detoxification is a rejuvenating treatment that originated in Southern India. The treatment was originally reserved for royalty and the wealthy. Pouches filled with herbs are soaked in hot water first and then warmed herbal oil and then gently swept across the body. The warmth of the treatment allows the skin to full absorb the herbal oils, enabling the nutrients to reach all the cells, making possible the removal of accumulated waste products. The lymphatic system is stimulated, the blood is cleansed, the immune system is enhanced and new white blood cells are produced.

What's New

Melanie Burns joined us as a full-time therapist in January of this year. She is a graduate of the Heritage Institute (formerly the Bodyworks Institute) in May 2002. She decided to go into massage because she has always enjoyed helping others. She specializes in Swedish, Deep Tissue and Pregnancy massage.

Nory Diaz graduated from the Potomac Massage Therapy Institute in February 2002. She joins our staff as a part-time therapist working Monday and Wednesday evenings. Her specialties are Swedish and Deep Tissue.

Libby Kaiser joins us part-time. She is a graduate of Baltimore School of Massage. Libby decided to go into massage because she recognized its power in preventing disease and illness. She has been practicing massage since the early 90s and uses the following modalities to help her clients release their pain: Swedish, Deep Tissue, Trigger Point, Shiatsu, Cranio-Sacral, and Myofascial.

Therapeutic Aromatherapy Study Group

Learn to apply the healing energies of essential oils. Sunday, March 16 from 2-4 p.m. Call Peggy to register on (703) 532-5192. $10 Donation

Tips and Tidbits

A tip from Ayurveda for creating self-health: Kapha season starts soon! Start taking Kapha-balancing measures now! Increase your warming and drying attributes in your clothing, your food, your spices, your environment. The number one Kapha-balancing spice to use is ginger. Add it to everything, even a few pieces of fresh ginger root in your water bottle, and reduce the effects of too much Kapha as all this snow becomes heavy, wet, and slows us down!

When shoveling snow, make sure that you are bending at the knees and not twisting your back. You should take several breaks and stretch.

Coaches Corner

Give yourself the give of health for 2003 with Health Coaching from MassageWorks. This package includes 2 1-hour massage, 2 Ayurvedic consultations and 2 telesuccess coaching session per month for $300 (a $420 value).

Health Coaching at MassageWorks: Perfect Health is as Easy as A, B, C! by Sally Toth, CPCC, CMT, ALC

How are you doing on your New Year's Resolutions? Were you one of the forty gazillion people who vowed that THIS YEAR would be the one you'd stick to a diet, lose some weight, create some more time for yourself, or go to the gym or that yoga class more regularly? I sure was. I'm sticking to my plan, I'm reaching my goals, and as a Health Coach, Massage Therapist, and Ayurvedic practitioner, I can show you how you can achieve your goals, too! It's as easy as A, B, C!

If you really want to change your situation, jump start your body's innate healing processes, and improve the quality of your life, consider using the new Health Coaching program at MassageWorks. This is the only program of its kind in the Metro DC area, because we are the only location that has an Ayurvedic Practitioner, a Massage Therapist, and a Certified Professional Coach all in one place--and all in one person!

First of all, let's go over the parts of this ABC Health Program. Its components are Ayurveda, Bodywork, and Coaching.

A: Ayurveda

Ayurveda is a comprehensive system of holistic health which developed in India about 5,000 years ago. It is the oldest, continuously-practiced healthcare system in the world, and it is endorsed by the World Health Organization. The amazing starting place is discovering your mind-body type according to this ancient system of holistic health. Several two-hour workshops are scheduled for this Spring term to introduce you to the principles and application of this amazingly simple and profoundly impactful way of life. Learn about *vata*, *pitta*, and *kapha*--what they are, how to pronounce all these words, and what they could mean for you in your life.

Have you felt an inordinate amount of stress lately (who hasn't!)? Has your sleep been interrupted or much deeper and prolonged than usual? Have you had difficulty losing weight? Have you been frustrated about not getting your life together? Ayurveda can address those issues through examining your lifestyle, your diet, your relationships and communication style, and how you react to stress and tension. Through the on-going application of Ayurvedic principles to all areas of your life, you can increase your energy, clarity, and mental focus. You'll approach life with a greater sense of balance and ease. Many of you will probably drop a few unwanted pounds. And for those who experience chronic pain, you can expect a reduction or elimination of that pain over time.

Working with an Ayurvedic Practitioner on a regular basis over the course of several months will provide you with the keys to living a longer, happier life as world events change, as we examine and shift our priorities, and as our bodies change with time. This is an exciting, dynamic health system that's fun to learn about, and it's individualized so it's convenient to apply to your existing lifestyle, and easy to customize for your individual needs.

B: Bodywork

As you all know, massage and other types of bodywork not only feel good, they're good for you and are an integral part of long-lasting health, both preventative and therapeutic. Through massage, reiki, body wraps, creative visualization, aromatherapy, and increasing your mind-body awareness, incredible healing takes place on many levels. Who hasn't experienced a greater sense of well-being and comfort in the rest of their lives through making on-going bodywork a part of their plan for health and wellness? If anyone says "Me! I haven't experienced that!", then you probably need to call and make an appointment more often! ☺

With the various therapists at MassageWorks, you'll be able to find exactly the right type of calming, relaxing, or energizing bodywork to balance your individual needs.

C: Coaching

This is a new term to some, in the way it is being presented here. I am referring to life coaching, with an emphasis on health. I believe, as do many of you, that when you're healthy, it creates and allows for possibilities of success in all other areas of your life. As a health coach, I help you design a program for achieving specific goals related initially to your health, and ultimately to every facet of your life. Through weekly appointments in person or via telephone, I will ask you questions to continuously clarify your priorities, goals, and values. I also use coaching tools and games to keep the learning fun, light, and all about you. A coach asks a lot of questions in order to help you find deeper answers to your own questions. Through coaching, you can expect to approach your life with more clarity and purpose, to find flexibility and various perspectives while exploring difficult issues, and to grow into the you whom you've always wanted to be. If you're feeling stuck, sick, or tired, enlist a coach to help you find the freedom to move along your life's path.

> MassageWorks is the only location in the Metro DC area which offers the unique combination of the ancient healing wisdom of Ayurvedic Lifestyle Consultations, the proven effectiveness of hands-on, healing Bodywork, and the empowerment of client-centered Health and Life Coaching.

> If you are seeking true healing and are committed to taking your life into your own hands, this is an unbeatable combination and an incredible value. Ayurveda, Bodywork, and Coaching are available as individual services or as a combination in economic and convenient packages.

The three-month package is for people who want better health and well-being, balance and choice, a sense of commitment and purpose to life, goal fulfillment, increased energy, weight and health maintenance, and the opportunity to live the life of your dreams.

We will begin with a one-hour health and wellness consultation to discuss your goals, what you want to change in your life and focus on during the on-going coaching sessions, get a sense of where you are and where you want to go, and to set up a schedule of appointments. We will set up a flexible schedule of 12 weeks (three months) of private one-on-one coaching, either in person or via telephone. (*You don't have to present to win!*)

In our first session together, we will create your Wheel of Life. Then hang on for the ride of your life! We'll create a travel agenda together, explore many of the following sites on the way to your dream life:

- ॐ Mining for Values
- ॐ Taming Your Gremlin
- ॐ Meeting Your Future Self
- ॐ Your Dream Life Vision
- ॐ Treasure Map of Perspectives
- ॐ Hero's Journey
- ॐ Guided Imagery
- ॐ Personal Nutrition

ॐ Simple Meditation
ॐ Crafting Your Life Purpose Statement
ॐ And whatever else you need to complete your journey

Coaching is for people who want to -- or are experiencing -- some change in their lives. A Coach asks questions to help you access your inner wisdom, believing that you have all the answers. A coach is also your biggest supporter and confidant, providing insight, support, motivation, and a professional and proven method to assist you in reaching your goals, whether they be in the area of health, career, finances, relationships, or a combination! We call this Co-Active Coaching because it is a process that is co-designed by coach and client together, with the focus on the client's goals and priorities.

Using Ayurveda, Bodywork, and Coaching, create customized solutions for time management, stress management and work/life balance needs. Unleash the power, creativity, and vitality within you to create the life you've always wanted. Call me at MassageWorks to answer any of your questions: 703-536-7200. Turn over a new leaf this Spring. Change your health and change your life.

Your coach at MassageWorks is Sally Toth, a Certified Professional Life and Health Coach, a Nationally Certified Massage therapist, and an Ayurvedic Lifestyle Consultant.

Schedule of Classes

Stretching and Sculpting Classes

Classes begin February 7 and end May 23, 2003. No classes the following dates: March 14, March 25-28. All classes are one hour.

Class Descriptions and Times

Yoga for Flexibility In this class, we will incorporate varied flowing mixture of stretches using yoga, the tennis ball and yoga strap created to lengthen your muscles increase flexibility and open your joints.
Wednesdays at 6:30 p.m. or Fridays at 8:30 a.m.

Butt and Gut In this class, we will focus on your abdominal and gluteal muscles. We will draw from Pilates, Yoga and traditional exercises to trim and tone.
Wednesdays at 8:30 a.m. or Thursdays at 6:30 p.m.

Total Body Sculpt This class intermixes standing, seated and floor exercises. You'll sculpt and tone your entire body using Yoga, Pilates and more traditional exercises using hand weights (you'll need to bring 1 to 5 lb. weights to class).
Tuesdays at 6:30 p.m.

Fee Schedule

One Class/Week $115; Two Classes/Week $220

Drop-in class for registered students: $9; non-registered students: $10. Please call first to make sure there is room to drop in. Missed classes can be made up at any time during the current session.

Refunds: We will refund fees prior to the beginning of the session minus a $15 administrative fee. After the session begins there are no refunds.

Registration

Mail or drop off your registration form to MassageWorks, 450 W. Broad St. Suite 412, Falls Church, VA 22046
Register with a credit card by calling MassageWorks at (703) 536-7200 or fax registration to (703) 536-1776 or on-line at linda@massageworksinc.com.

Workshops

Ayurvedic Nutrition - This advanced class will go into the fine--and fun!--points of healthy cooking, using the balancing, health-creating principles of Ayurveda. Create your own, personalized, healthy eating plan. Ayurveda is a 5,000-year-old system of health and balance which originated in India and is the world's oldest continuously-practiced medicine.
Instructor: Sally Toth   Cost: $25
Dates: February 8, 1 – 3 p.m. or March 15, 1 – 3 p.m.

Creating Balance and Fulfillment in Your Life - Would you like to have more time to spend with family and friends? A fresh perspective on what's important in your life? Clarity and insight about the choices you make? A compelling way to say "YES!" to energy boosters and "NO!" to energy drainers? Come to this two-hour workshop designed to help you discover and stay committed to your core values, create more balance in your life and make room for what you really want to be doing.
Instructor: Sally Toth   Cost: $25
Dates: January 18, 10 a.m. – noon or May 17, 10 a.m. - noon

Creating Healthy, Balanced Relationships - Ever wonder why you "click" with some people and not with others? You will experience many "aha!" moments in this workshop and will leave armed with tools to achieve great communication, love, and trust in all your relationships. *"Intro to Ayurveda" strongly recommended prior to taking this course.*
Instructor: Sally Toth   Cost: $25
Dates: May 3   Time: 10 a.m. - noon

Introduction to Ayurveda - Create balance, health, and happiness in your life, based on your mind-body type. Learn to make choices that will result in success, in a way that is most natural for you. Choose the perfect diet, exercise, career, relationships, and more! Ayurveda is a 5,000-year-old system of health and balance which originated in India and is the world's oldest continuously-practiced medicine.

Instructor: Sally Toth   Cost: $25
Dates: February 8, 10 a.m. – noon or March 15, 10 a.m. - noon

If I Only Knew Now...Meeting Your Future Self - Discover what you need to know now to get you where you want to be. Wouldn't it be great if you could tap into the wisdom of the person you will be twenty years from now? This is your chance, and this is your life. Learn how to make the very best of it through a unique perspective. Bring pencil and paper, or a journal.

Instructor: Sally Toth   Cost: $25
Dates: January 21, 7-9 p.m. or March 1, 10 a.m. - noon

Reiki I - History and principles of Reiki are taught and techniques for using Reiki on yourself and others. By the end of class, you are able to do a complete Reiki session.

Instructor: Linda Steele   Cost: $150
Dates: March 8 or May 31   Time: 10 a.m. to 4 p.m.

Reiki II – For those who wish to further their Reiki experience. Participants learn to use Reiki over a distance (i.e. the recipient doesn't have to be present to receive treatment) and sacred symbols to enhance a Reiki session.

Instructor: Linda Steele   Cost: $150
Dates: April 12 or Jun 14   Time: 10 a.m. to 4 p.m.

Taming Your Gremlin - Move beyond your Inner Critic to create the life you REALLY want. Meet the "voices in your head" that keep you from living a joyful life, and learn what they're trying to tell you. Based on *Taming Your Gremlin*™ by Richard D. Carson.

Instructor: Sally Toth   Cost: $25
Dates: February 22, 10 a.m. – noon or May 17, 1 – 3 p.m.

To register for workshops:

Mail or drop off your registration form to MassageWorks, 450 W. Broad St., Suite 412, Falls Church, VA 22046.
You may also register with a credit card by calling MassageWorks at (703) 536-7200 or fax registration to (703) 536-1776 or on-line at linda@massageworksinc.com.

a carol on Stretching Yourself by Carol Goldsmith

The class schedule listed Power Yoga at 8 am. Hmmm, that sounds interesting.
I've never done yoga before. It looks so relaxing and fluid on TV that it doesn't seem like exercise. Yet here it is at the health club. I'll head over to Studio B.

A young Japanese man with contoured muscles and trim goatee stands next to a gigantic black boom box. Heads are bobbing to the synthetic beat. I take a spot in the back row behind one of those purple plastic aerobic steps. Fortunately, it's right next to the door.

My head starts bobbing along with the class. I thought yoga music was soft and calm tinkling bells and waterfalls. But hey, the class is called Power Yoga so I guess we're supposed to pump it up.

The instructor leads us through a series of poses. We reach, we punch, we form a human bow and arrow. So far so good. The music intensifies along with the moves. We step up and down on the aerobic platforms, faster and faster, then we kick.

Hmmm, this is seeming less like yoga by the minute and more like the Radio City Rockettes. I'm surprised at how high my legs go.

I keep stepping and kicking as sweat beads start rolling down my back. I'm already drained at half past eight. The instructor leaps and two dozen leotards fly through the air like the cast in a kung fu movie.

My heart is beating out of my chest. Maybe yoga isn't my cup of herbal tea.

I grab my empty Evian bottle and head for the fountain outside Studio B, knowing that I won't be back. Damn, I can't even make it through a whole yoga class. I'm in a lot worse shape than I thought.

I walk down the hall past Studio A, where I hear the sound of tinkling bells. There in a darkened room, I can just make out twenty slender silhouettes slowly and gently stretching their limbs. I check the class schedule. That's my Power Yoga class! Where in the heck was I?

I scan the listing for Studio B. I was in Aerobic Kickboxing!
I'm laughing at this sudden kick in the pants, when I realize something important. I was doing pretty darn well at Aerobic Kickboxing for never having kick-boxed before. Instead of feeling like a failure, I suddenly feel like a raging success. I succeeded in stretching my comfort zone.

Where in your life could you make a stretch?

Pick something of interest that you've never done. Then sign up for a class, go to a meeting, or join a group to check it out. Enter the room with beginner's mind. Instead of comparing yourself to everyone else ("They know more than I do. They're experienced. They're better than I am. I look like a fool."), keep your comparisons to yourself. Compare your feelings at the end of the experience to how you felt when you went in.

Did you stretch yourself? Did you enjoy the stretch? Are you expanding your comfort zone?

We grow in life by exercising more courage and less self-doubt. Decide this week to do something new. There's incredible power in stretching yourself.

Contact Us

We would love to hear your input about our newsletter. This is a free service from MassageWorks intended to inform and enlighten you regarding some of our services and other beneficial health information. Let us know what you think. Thanks so much! You can reach us at linda@massageworksinc.com

Disclaimer

MassageWorks respects your time and privacy; so if you do NOT wish to receive this newsletter, please reply with "unsubscribe" in the body of your message.
We will remove you from our list as quickly as possible. If you know of anyone who would LIKE to be added to our e-mail list, please contact us with their information or have them contact us at: info@massageworksinc.com.

Sample Press Release

MassageWorks, Inc.
450 W. Broad Street, Suite 412
Falls Church, Virginia 22046
(703) 536-7200

Contact: Linda Steele
(703) 536-7200

For Immediate Release

IS STRESS MAKING YOU CROOKED?
MASSAGEWORKS CELEBRATES THEIR SECOND ANNIVERSARY WITH FREE
POSTURAL ANALYSIS SCREENINGS

Falls Church, VA – October 3, 2002 – "Most people are crooked and don't even know it," says MassageWorks' owner Linda Steele, who has worked with hundreds of stressed individuals during her 3-year career in massage therapy. "Headaches, backaches, uneven shoulders – all are signs that stress may be getting the better of someone," she says. "It's amazing how the human body responds to stress, and long term, how that stress impacts a person's health."

To celebrate its two-year anniversary helping people take better care of themselves, MassageWorks, a company who has been serving the Northern Virginia area with massage therapy, facials, body treatments and nail care, is inviting the public to an Open House celebration featuring free postural analysis screenings, seated massage, healthy cooking demonstrations and lectures on Stress Management, Introduction to Ayurveda, Creating Balance and Fulfillment Through Coaching and Self-Health Through Food: Your Kitchen Pharmacy.

The Open House will be held on Sunday, October 20 from 2:00 – 4:00 p.m. at 450 W. Broad Street, Suite 412, Falls Church, VA 22046. For more information, call (703) 536-7200.

# # #

Business, Marketing and Life Coaches

Lorri Bein
E-mail: lorrib@tonyrobbins.com
(562) 438-5560

Nina East
The Follow-Through Coach
www.ninaeast.com
E-mail: nina@ninaeast.com
(919) 967-3144

Carol Goldsmith
The Discovery Coach
www.carolgoldsmith.com
E-mail: carol@carolgoldsmith.com
(703) 860-6178

Linda Steele
The Business of Massage
(703) 536-7200

Chapter 8 - Get Out There and Talk

Voice Coach

Sally Toth
www.personalprism.com
E-mail: sally@personalprism.com
(703) 912-2901

Toastmasters
www.toastmasters.org

The Sound of Your Voice by Dr. Carol Fleming
Audio Partners, Auburn CA
Available at Amazon and local book stores

Chapter 9 - Public Relations and Publicity

Directories

Power Media Selects
2333 Wisconsin Ave., NW
Washington, D.C. 20007
(202) 333-4904
The best directory on the market, available in three-ring volume or on floppy disk.

Editor & Publisher
11 W. 19th Street
New York, NY 10011
(212) 675-4380
Superb listing, especially of daily newspapers across North America. Also contains weeklies, college papers, African-American newspapers, syndicates and much more. Updated annually.

Bacon's Publicity Checker
332 S. Michigan Ave.
Chicago, IL 60604
(800) 621-0561
Similar to Editor & Publisher. Bacon's has several volumes covering print and electronic media. An excellent directory.

BPI Media Services
1695 Oak Street
Lakewood, NJ 08701
(800) 753-6675
BPI offer several directories: radio, TV, cable, syndicated columnists, TV news, and news bureaus. Comprehensive and easy to read but expensive.

Gebbie Press
Box 1000
New Paltz, NY 12561
(914) 255-7560
Over 21,000 listings. All American daily papers, weeklies, TV and radio, consumer magazines, business press, ethic press, you name it. And it's

less expensive than other directories. Comes in 500-page spiral-bound volume or floppy disk.

Writer's Marketing
1507 Dana Ave.
Cincinnati, OH 45207
Over 4,000 listings to help you sell what you write. Valuable information about scores of specialized publications.

Directory of Experts, Authorities, and Spokesperson
2233 Wisconsin Avenue, NW #540
Washington, D.C. 20007
(202) 333-4904
This is a directory you want to be in. Write or call for information on how you can be included. It will cost you a few hundred dollars to run your advertisement. This could be your ticket to bookings on TV and radio talk shows.

Newsmaker Interviews
8217 Beverly Rd.
Los Angeles, CA 90048
This newsletter will include you in its monthly listing as a potential talk show guest.

Public Relations Firm

Steve Winter
Brotman, Winter, Fried Communications
111 Park Place
Falls Church, VA 22046
(703) 536-3600

Chapter 13 – Web sites

Jim Green
OpenNet
www.theinternetutility.net
E-mail: jimgreen@opennetworks.com
(703) 923-0097
(877) 876-3379

Suggested Reading

Feng Shui and Space Clearning

Collins, Terah Kathryn. The Western Guide to Feng Shui. Carlsbad, CA: Hay House, 1996.

Kingston, Karen. Clear Your Clutter with Feng Shui. New York, NY: Broadway Books, 1999.

Kingston, Karen. Creating Sacred Space with Feng Shui. New York, NY: Broadway Books, 1997.

Linn, Denise. Sacred Space. Ballentine Books, 1996.

Mantras

Ashley-Farrand, Thomas. *The Power of Mantras.* Boulder, CO: Sounds True, Inc., 1999.

Marketing and Sales

Gitomer, Jeffrey. *The Sales Bible.* New York, New York: William Morrow Company, Inc., 1994.

Levinson, Jay Conrad. *Guerrilla Marketing.* New York, New York: Houghton Mifflin Co., 1994.

Metaphysical Teachings

Butterworth, Eric. *Spiritual Economics.* Unity Village, MO: Unity School of Christianity, 1983.

Murphy, Joseph. How to Use the Laws of Mind. Marina del Rey, CA: DeVorss & Company, 1980.

Murphy, Joseph. *Your Infinite Power to be Rich.* Paramus, NJ: Prentice-Hall, 1966.

Murphy, Joseph. *The Cosmic Power Within You.* West Nyack, NY: Parker Publishing Company, 1968.

Murphy, Joseph. The Power of Your Subconscious Mind. Engle Cliffs, NJ: Prentice-Hall, 1963.

Ponder, Catherine. *Open Your Mind to Prosperity.* Marina del Ray, CA: DeVorss & Company, 1971 and 1983.

Ponder, Catherine. *The Dynamic Laws of Prosperity.* Marina del Ray, CA: DeVorss & Company, 1962 and 1985.

Ponder, Catherine. *The Prosperity Secrets of the Ages.* Marina del Ray, CA: DeVorss & Company, 1964 and 1986.

Publicity and Public Relations

Parkhurst, William. *How to Get Publicity.* New York, NY: HarperCollins, 2000.

Self-help/Psychology/Inspiration

Grabhorn, Lynn. *Excuse Me, Your Life is Waiting.* Charlottesville, VA: Hampton Roads Publishing Company, Inc., 2000.

Robbins, Anthony. *Awaken the Giant Within.* New York, NY: Simon and Schuster, 1991.

Robbins, Anthony. *Unlimited Power.* New York, NY: Simon and Schuster, 1986.

Roger, John and Peter McWilliams. You Can't Afford the Luxury of a Negative Thought. Los Angeles, CA: Prelude Press, 1988.

Schwartz, David, PhD. *The Magic of Thinking Big.* New York, NY: Simon & Schster, 1987

Voice Coaching

Fleming, Carol, PhD. The Sound of Your Voice. Auburn, CA: Audio Partners, 1986.

Notes

Chapter 2 – Marketing Plan

Levinson, Jay Conrad. *Guerrilla Marketing.* New York, New York: Houghton Mifflin Co., 1994, p. 4

Chapter 6 – Networking

Gitomer, Jeffrey. *The Sales Bible.* New York, New York: William Morrow Company, Inc.,1994, page 263.

Chapter 17 - Out into the Universe

Ashley-Farrand, Thomas. *The Power of Mantras.* Boulder, CO: Sounds True, Inc., 1999, page 5.

Collins, Terah Kathryn. The Western Guide to Feng Shui. Carlsbad, CA: Hay House, 1996, page 8.

Chapter 18 - Magnetizing Yourself

Murphy, Joseph. The Power of Your Subconscious Mind. Engle Cliffs, NJ: Prentice-Hall, 1963, pages 22 and 128.

Afterword

Ponder, Catherine. *The Prosperity Secrets of the Ages.* Marina del Ray, CA: DeVorss & Company, 1964 and 1986, p. 328.

About the Author

Linda Steele is a trainer, consultant and successful business owner. Graduating from Marymount University with a B.B.A. in International Business, she has over 10 years of training, development and management expertise gained while working for DocuPro, a financial data company. She is an entrepreneur and business owner, serving as President/CEO of MassageWorks, Inc. and The Business of Massage.

Linda has completed training to practitioner level in Neuro Linguistic Programming (NLP – the technology of how people think, behave and achieve excellence) which provides an important grounding in the dynamics of personal change and achievement. She is a graduate of Tony Robbins' Mastery University.